6/20

God In Me

God In Me

A Popular Explanation of Sanctifying Grace
or the Mystery of God's Life in Us

by
MATTHEW M. SWIZDOR, O.F.M.Conv.

Preface by
HIS EXCELLENCY, LAWRENCE J. SHEHAN, D.D.
Bishop of Bridgeport

Illustrated by
KAY B. LEITTEN

Published by
THE FRANCISCAN FATHERS, O.F.M.Conv.
St. Hyacinth College and Seminary
Granby, Massachusetts

Nihil obstat (pro Ordine):
> GREGORY GRABKA, S.T.D., O.F.M.CONV.

Imprimi potest:
> GEORGE ROSKWITALSKI, S.T.D., O.F.M.CONV.
> *Provincial*

Nihil obstat:
> WILLIAM F. KEARNEY
> *Censor librorum*

Imprimatur:
> ✠ LAWRENCE J. SHEHAN, D.D.
> *Bishop of Bridgeport*

Bridgeport, August 1, 1957

THIRD PRINTING

PRINTED
IN
U. S. A.

DEDICATION

*This book is dedicated to the Son of God
who became the Son of Man
in order that sons of men
might become sons of God.*

CONTENTS

CONTENTS

PREFACE

Nothing is so important to the soul as sanctifying grace; yet nothing is more difficult than the task of imparting to people, especially to children, an effective knowledge of the meaning and importance of this divine gift. In undertaking to supply a practical exemplification of the way in which the meaning and reality of such grace can be brought home even to children, Father Matthew has undertaken a most useful piece of work.

Father Matthew's skill as a catechist is born of his native ability and the loving devotion he has given to many years of experience in instructing children in the truths of their religion. The time and care he has lavished on this little book are immediately evident, and reflect his own love of God, his affection for the children he serves, and his devotion to the great work of the catechist.

What characterizes this book is the profuse but clear and apt use of many of the illustrations found in Holy Scripture to explain the significance and effectiveness of sanctifying grace, and the ingenious experiments he has worked out to imprint these things indelibly on the mind. All will recognize the necessary imperfections in the parallel between such material experiments and the sublime spiritual operations they illustrate. But in the hands of the intelligent reader or skilled catechist this need not detract from their usefulness.

All who read and use this book will recognize that it is a work of love. In authorizing its publication it is my hope that it may produce abundant fruits of the Christian love that inspired it, preparing the souls of many for the fuller participation in that sanctifying grace which is its theme.

LAWRENCE J. SHEHAN, D.D.
Bishop of Bridgeport

AUTHOR'S INTRODUCTION

1. This volume is an outgrowth of a little booklet entitled GOD IN ME AND I IN HIM, printed in 1950. The booklet was originally intended for the private use of the author in instructing young people in the difficult subject of sanctifying grace. It was subsequently released to the public, though in a limited way, because of its proved effectiveness. Despite the fact that comparatively little effort was made to make the booklet known, numerous orders were received from various parts of the country. We were especially impressed by the fact that hundreds of copies were ordered and reordered by priests and seminarians. The merits of the booklet were extolled spontaneously and requests were received for a larger, more complete edition. We hope that this book is the answer to that request.

2. FOR CHILDREN AND ADULTS. The original booklet was intended for children in the fourth grade and up, and was juvenile in character. Learning, however, that many adults, especially educators, were interested in the work, we decided to make this book more suitable for adult reading, while keeping it simple enough to be understood, for the most part, by children in the upper grades. Not all the material may be equally suited for every age-group, but the number and variety of the stories ensure every reader or instructor a good choice of suitable material. In fact, we have learned from experience that most of the material will interest adults as much as, or even more than, children. The footnotes, as one can readily guess, are intended for adults.

3. ASSOCIATION OF IDEAS. The function of the book lies chiefly in impressing the mind with an interesting and absorbing, down-to-earth fact, and then associating this fact with a supernatural truth. The mysteries of faith, often cold and obscure to the mind because of their abstractness, thus become almost as interesting, colorful, clear and unforgettable as the examples themselves. On a number of occasions, for example, after seeing the charcoal experiment (Chapter VIII) performed only once, fourth-grade pupils were able to explain it in detail, giving the correct meaning of each step.

4. WIDE RANGE OF USEFULNESS. Originally this book, developed in the classroom, was intended primarily for classroom use, but this in no way lessens its usefulness outside the classroom. It can be understood quite easily by pupils of the upper grades, and its content can be taught with even greater success to high-school students and older groups. Preachers will be able to make use of much of the material in sermons. And everyone will find in the volume a wealth of material for pious meditation.

5. "IF THEY ONLY KNEW!" How different the world would be if people only realized and appreciated their dignity as children of God! But, unfortunately, most of them have only a vague notion of this ineffable mystery. What can be done about it? Teach them about sanctifying grace? To be sure—but the very mention of the word "sanctifying grace" is discouraging. A fine tool for the use of the trained theologian, the term is too abstract and obscure for the layman: like the veil over the face of Moses, it hides the splendor of God's wondrous gift.[1]

---

[1] "We do not act as Moses did, who used to put a veil over his face that the Israelites might not observe the glory of his countenance."—2 Corinthians 3, 13. See also verses 7-11; and Exodus 34, 29-35.

6. SANCTIFYING GRACE IS LIFE. Christ, the greatest teacher, did not use technical terms in His teachings, but He made Himself understood as no one else ever could. He spoke of sanctifying grace simply as "life"—His life in us. St. John, His beloved Apostle, understood this perhaps better than anyone else. He tells us that he wrote his Gospel in order that we may have *life* through our belief that Jesus is the Christ.[2] In the very first chapter of his Gospel, St. John says: "In Him was *life,* and the *life* was the light of men."[3] Then he speaks of "the power of becoming sons of God" by being *"born* . . . of God."[4] In the third chapter he lets the words of the Master explain that one is born of God through "water and the Spirit."[5] And in subsequent chapters he continues to unfold before us in Christ's own words the great mystery of the *life* that we have from God through Christ: *everlasting life,* the only life really worthy of the name. In the fourth chapter, for example, we read of the fountain of *living water* springing up in our hearts unto *life everlasting.*[6] And in the sixth chapter we read of the *bread of life,* the *living bread* which preserves this everlasting life in us.[7]

These are but a few examples. One needs only to read the Gospel and First Epistle of St. John with an eye open for the word "life" to be convinced that this was Christ's own best name for sanctifying grace. And what name could be more appropriate? After all, is not our natural life but an imitation of the real, eternal life which God shares with us in the *super*-natural order? Reflect, for example, on this combination of Christ's words: "I came

---

2 John 20, 31.
3 John 1, 4.
4 John 1, 12-13.
5 John 3, 5.
6 John 4, 14.
7 John 6, 27-59.

that they may have *life,* and have it more abundantly."[8] "For as the Father has *life* in Himself, even so He has given to the Son also to have *life* in Himself."[9] "And as I *live* because of the Father, so he who eats Me, he also shall *live* because of Me."[10] Reflect also on these words of St. John: "God has given us *eternal life;* and this life is in His Son. He who has the Son has the *life.* He who has not the Son has not the life."[11]

7. "GOD IN ME." But Christ had another expression for sanctifying grace, a more descriptive one. It appears a number of times in St. John and has inspired the title of this book. That it means the same as "life" can be seen from these two parallel sentences: "He who eats My flesh and drinks My blood *has life everlasting* . . . He who eats My flesh, and drinks My blood, ABIDES IN ME AND I IN HIM."[12] How much warmer and more inspiring, than the cold technical name we commonly use, are either of the above expressions of the Master! Suppose that He had said instead: He who eats My flesh and drinks My blood has sanctifying grace!

8. SIMPLE TERMS. In this book, written primarily for God's "little ones," whether young or old, simple or learned, we have tried to imitate the Master by explaining in simple terms that sanctifying grace is a *new life* in our souls through our sharing in the very *life* and *divine nature* of God Himself,[13] and that this new life is in us not as if we were merely

---

8 John 10, 10.
9 John 5, 26.
10 John 6, 58.
11 1 John 5, 11-12.
12 John 6, 55, 57.
13 "He has granted us the very great and precious promises, so that through them you may become **partakers of the divine nature,** having escaped from the corruption of that lust which is in the world." —2 Peter 1, 4.

its container, but as our own second and more excellent nature, *super*-nature, to be exact. But, if it is difficult to make any hard thing easy, it is much more so to make sanctifying grace—difficult enough for theologians—easily understandable to people not trained in theology, and especially to children. In a work of this kind, one has to be content with the degree of precision afforded by more simple terms.

9. THE EXPERIMENTS. Chapter VIII was composed especially for classroom use. Whenever it is so used, the experiments should be performed if possible. They are easy and very interesting, and interest is a guarantee of lasting impressions on the minds of the pupils. These impressions, when properly associated with the spiritual truths they are made to represent, make the latter not only understandable but also quite unforgettable.

10. EQUIPMENT. Most of the equipment necessary for the experiments can be found in rectories, convents or schools. The rest can be borrowed from laboratories or pupils' chemistry sets, or purchased from a scientific equipment store or through one's pharmacist.

11. THE CHARCOAL EXPERIMENT is performed just as easily as it appears in the book, provided certain laws of physics are observed. The charcoal, being black and heat-absorbent, ignites readily with the help of any ordinary magnifying glass. Although any cheap magnifying glass will do, results will be better and more certain if a good magnifying glass is available, especially if the sunlight is weak, on account of atmospheric conditions such as smoke, haze, etc. Common window glass, if clean, is usually no hindrance, but window screens or curtains decrease the intensity of the sun's radi-

ation to a very noticeable degree, making it difficult to ignite the charcoal. On a clear day, with a good magnifying glass, the experiment works like magic. Care should be taken to hold the magnifying glass at right angles to the path of sunlight and at such a distance—usually a few inches—from the charcoal that the converging rays of the sun form the smallest and brightest point possible upon the charcoal. A prudent instructor will try each experiment privately before attempting to perform it in public.

12. OXYGEN. One may have more difficulty in obtaining the equipment and material for the oxygen experiment. Be sure that the rubber tube and connecting tubes are not blocked, thus preventing the free flow of oxygen. WARNING: Be sure to put a short piece of glass or metal tubing at the free end of the rubber tube; otherwise, the intense heat from the charcoal may cause the rubber to ignite and burn explosively, since that end of the tube must be held quite close (about one inch) to the burning coal. After the experiment, the chemicals will usually be found caked hard in the test tube, but plain water will dissolve them readily after the tube has cooled. The purpose of this experiment is to explain the increase of sanctifying grace in a very interesting and impressive manner, as will be indicated. But if it should be impossible or impractical to perform it, the instructor can fan the charcoal or blow upon it, explaining that this forces more oxygen from the air against the fire, thus making it burn more intensely. The principle is the same, though the effect be less impressive and, consequently, more easily forgotten.

13. MEANS TO AN END. The experiments are only an interesting means to an end, the successful attainment of which will depend upon the instructor.

14. We hope that this book will—we know it can—help many people to better understand and appreciate God's greatest gift to man, a real share in His own divine life and nature.

—FR. MATTHEW

"And passing by thee,
I saw that thou wast
trodden under foot
in thy own blood,
and I said to thee..
LIVE." EZECHIEL 16,6.

Chapter I

HEAVENLY PRINCES AND PRINCESSES

God Tells a Story

Many years ago, before Christ was born, God often spoke to mankind through holy men called prophets. Many of the things He said are now contained in the Holy Bible. One of these prophets was Ezechiel. In the sixteenth chapter of his book of prophecies he tells us a story about a baby girl who had been abandoned by her mother and left to die by the wayside. Fortunately, a great king was passing by and, seeing the baby he had pity on her; carrying her home he took care of her and brought her up like a princess. And when she had grown up he made her his own bride and queen.

God does not tell stories in the Bible to amuse people, but to teach them spiritual lessons. Many of these stories mean something different besides what they actually say. We call them allegories or parables. Jesus often used such stories to explain His teachings. Thus, in the story related by Ezechiel, God is actually telling us how He took care of, protected, and glorified the city of Jerusalem and the Hebrew people. For, the baby girl in the story is Jerusalem and the king is God Himself.

The story, with God Himself as narrator, reads in part as follows: "And passing by thee, I saw that thou wast trodden under foot in thy own blood, and I said to thee . . . : *Live.* . . . And I washed thee with water, and cleansed away thy blood from thee, and I anointed thee with oil. And I clothed thee with embroidery, and shod thee with violet-

[1]

colored shoes; and I girded thee with fine garments. I decked thee also with ornaments, and put bracelets on thy hands, and a chain about thy neck. And I put a jewel upon thy forehead and earrings in thy ears, and a beautiful crown upon thy head. And thou wast adorned with gold and silver, and wast clothed with fine linen, and embroidered work, and many colors. Thou didst eat fine flour, and honey, and oil, and wast made exceeding beautiful, and wast advanced to be a queen. And thy renown went forth among the nations for thy beauty, for *thou wast perfect through my beauty, which I had put upon thee,* saith the Lord God."[1]

In Our Own Times

The story of Ezechiel was the inspiration for a similar story which I am going to tell you now, a story which speaks of truly wonderful things which have happened in our own times. Here now is our story:

A few years ago, a little baby was abandoned by its heartless parents in a dark city park. It could not speak or walk or even raise its little head, for it was still too weak, having been born but a few days before. Cold and hungry, it could only shiver and cry in the blackness of the night. As it lay there crying, a great king came by, taking his evening walk. Hearing the feeble crying, he came closer till he could faintly see the baby in the darkness. We might think that he would have called his servants to pick it up and to carry it off to an orphanage. But not this king! He knelt beside the baby and, feeling great pity for it, he took it up gently into his arms and carried it to his palace. There he fed the baby, gave it a good warm bath, dressed it in fine clothes, and rocked it to sleep in his arms. By now he had grown so fond of the baby that he decided to keep it.

---

1 Ezechiel 16, 6-14.

[2]

And although he already had a son of his own, he adopted the poor little foundling and made it his own prince, as if it were his second son.

That lucky child is still living today, and so is the king. Who are they? The king is the great King of heaven and earth, God Himself. And the foundling? It is you—and I! Yes, each one of us is the lucky child who had been abandoned by our first parents, Adam and Eve, to die an everlasting death, but was rescued by our divine Saviour and made a great prince (or princess). You probably do not remember when it happened, because you were too young at the time; but it did happen—on the day of your Baptism. You were nestled in your godmother's arms, wrapped in warm blankets, perhaps sleeping peacefully. But your poor little soul was not so fortunate; for when you were born you already had an ugly sin on your soul, which we call original sin. Your soul was doomed to the darkness of never-ending spiritual death.[2] But at the moment of your Baptism, God came into the cold darkness of your soul, and by a very special gift which we call "sanctifying grace," He washed away that frightful sin. And, looking upon you with great pity, God said to you, as He did long ago to the baby girl in the story of Ezechiel, *"Live!"* And live you did! The everlasting death to which your soul had been condemned disappeared from your soul and you began to live a *new life*. New health and strength of soul became yours. Your soul not only became clean and beautiful, but it actually began

---

[2] The Council of Florence defined that those who die with only original sin and no personal mortal sins on their souls are condemned. (Denzinger-Banwart, Enchiridion Symbolorum, 410). The punishment of such souls, however, consists only in the privation of the vision of God. They do not suffer the pains of hell meted out to those who have committed personal mortal sins. For this reason we commonly call their state "limbo" rather than "hell." Though most theologians are of the opinion that souls in limbo enjoy a certain natural happiness, it is nevertheless a state of punishment.

to look like God Himself.[3] And when God saw how beautiful your soul was, He loved it greatly, and in a spiritual way, He, the great King of heaven, took it up into His arms, held it close to His heart, and made it His very own. Thus you—each one of us—became in all truth an adopted child of God, His heavenly prince or princess.[4]

We Were Born Twice

Wonderful as this story sounds, it is also true, for God Himself has revealed it. Thus in the Gospel of St. John the Holy Spirit tells us that Jesus came into the world to give to those who believe in Him *the power of becoming sons of God.*[5]

One evening when Nicodemus came to Jesus to talk with Him about the kingdom of God, Jesus said to him, "Amen, amen, I say to thee, unless a man be *born again,* he cannot see the kingdom of God." Nicodemus was puzzled and asked, "How can a man be born when he is old?" And Jesus answered, "Amen, amen, I say to thee, unless a man be *born again* of *water* and the *Spirit,* he cannot enter into the kingdom of God."[6] Unlike Nicodemus, we know that Jesus was speaking of Baptism. For it is through Baptism

3 Man's spiritual and immortal soul, endowed with intelligence and free will, makes him more like God than any other earthly creature. But this natural "likeness" unto God pales into insignificance when compared to the likeness unto God produced in the soul by sanctifying grace. The human soul, even with its superior natural faculties, is but a feeble, created imitation of God's transcendent nature. Sanctifying grace, on the other hand, gives the soul a real participation in the uncreated nature of God. This not only makes the soul "like to Him," but will also enable it, in heaven, to "see Him just as He is." — 1 John 3, 2.

4 "You have received a spirit of adoption as sons, by virtue of which we cry, 'Abba! Father!' The Spirit himself gives testimony to our spirit that we are sons of God. But if we are sons, we are heirs also: heirs indeed of God and joint heirs with Christ." —Romans 8, 15-17. See also Galatians 4, 4-7.

5 "But to as many as received Him he gave the power of becoming sons of God; to those who believe in His name: who were born not of blood, nor of the will of the flesh, nor of the will of man, but of God." —John 1, 12-13.

6 John 3, 3-5.

that we are "born again of water and the Spirit." At the moment the water of Baptism is poured over our body, the Holy Spirit comes into our soul, takes away our sins, and gives us a new and heavenly life. This life is a real and actual *sharing in God's own life,* the very life which God has in Himself from all eternity.[7] And since we now have a new life which we did not have before our Baptism, we can truly say that we were born twice: first of our parents, and then of God; first for the world, in a natural way, and then for heaven, in a spiritual or *super*natural way. People who have not been baptized are not children of God but are just plain human beings with no right to heaven.

The loveliest story the world has ever heard is the story of the birth of Jesus in Bethlehem. The tender beauty of the Christmas story proceeds from the fact that before Jesus was born of Mary He had already been born of God the Father from all eternity and was therefore the eternal Son of God.[8] And to think that through the grace of Baptism each one of us has been made to share, in some small measure at least, in the sublime dignity of the Son of God by being born of God! What a wonderful privilege! This does not mean, of course, that we are or ever could be equal to Jesus. For He is the natural Son of God, while we are God's adopted children; He is true God, while we are and always shall be only human. Our sharing in God's life through sanctifying grace makes our souls *like* God,[9] but it does not change us into God or make us equal to Him.

---

7 "He has granted us the very great and precious promises, so that through them you may become **partakers of the divine nature.**" —2 Peter 1, 4. See also Ephesians 4, 17-18.

8 The Father did not exist before the Son. The Three Persons of God are equally eternal. From all eternity the Son is born of the Father, and the Holy Ghost proceeds from both the Father and the Son.

9 "And He said: Let us make man to our **image and likeness** . . . And God created man to His own image." —Genesis 1, 26 and 27.

Among the many great kings, emperors, and rulers of history, there is one who seems to stand out above all others in glory. That king is Solomon, a monarch so great in wealth, in power, and in wisdom that his kingdom seems like a lovely vision from fairyland. The secret of his greatness lay in a dream or vision which he once had from God. In the dream King Solomon asked God for the gift of wisdom that he might govern his people wisely. And God granted his wish, saying: "Behold I have done for thee according to thy words, and have given thee a wise and understanding heart, insomuch that there hath been no one like thee before thee, nor shall arise after thee."[10] "And I will give thee riches, and wealth, and glory, so that none of the kings before thee, or after thee, shall be like thee."[11] The Holy Bible speaks at length of the fabulous riches, glory, and earthly wisdom of Solomon.[12] During his reign, Jerusalem abounded in gold, while silver became as plentiful as stones. Kings and wise men came even from distant lands to hear his wisdom and to see his great riches. The famed queen of Sheba came too, and was breathless with astonishment at the splendor of his kingdom.

Solomon's Downfall

Solomon was a very good king, too, when he was young. He loved and honored God and built a most beautiful temple for Him in Jerusalem, the splendor of which shall be proclaimed to the end of time. But Solomon had too many of the good things of life, and these made him become soft and spineless. Finally, he became so morally weak that

---

[10] 3 Kings 3, 12.

[11] 2 Paralipomenon 1, 12.

[12] For a better appreciation of this and the next paragraph, read the following in the Holy Bible: 3 Kings, chapters 3-11 and/or 2 Paralipomenon, chapters 1-9.

he even permitted idolatry and other great evils to spread in his kingdom. This made God very angry and He rebuked Solomon, but Solomon would not listen. In the end, God sent him many troubles and sufferings, and Solomon died an unhappy man. We do hope that he was truly sorry for his sins before he died and that God forgave him, for otherwise he could not have saved his soul.[13] And if he did not get to heaven, what did it profit him to have been such a glorious earthly king? For, as Jesus said, "What does it profit a man, if he gain the whole world, but suffer the loss of his own soul?"[14]

We Are Greater than Solomon

The earthly glory of kings lasts but a short time at best. Then they, like all men, die and most of them are soon forgotten. But the glory of the soul can never die as long as we remain faithful to God, for we are not earthly princes and princesses, but heavenly ones, children of the King of kings. And when our bodies die someday, our souls will only be beginning to truly live; for it is after death that God will give us His beautiful heaven and clothe us with the wondrous glory of heavenly princes and princesses— not just for a short lifetime, but forever.

Jesus once praised the Queen of Sheba who had come "from the ends of the earth to hear the wisdom of Solomon." And then, referring to Himself, He said, "and behold, a greater than Solomon is here."[15] Jesus never wore a jeweled crown on His head (though He wore a thorned one on the cross). He had no luxurious palace with countless servants

---

[13] Jesus said: "Children, with what difficulty will they who trust in riches enter the kingdom of God! It is easier for a camel to pass through the eye of a needle, than for a rich man to enter the kingdom of God." —Mark 10, 24-25. He also said: "Unless you repent, you will all perish." —Luke 13, 3. Opinion is divided concerning Solomon's salvation: some think that he was condemned, others hold that he found mercy before God.

[14] Matthew 16, 26.

[15] Matthew 12, 42.

to wait on Him. On the contrary, He was so poor during His public life, that He once said: "The foxes have dens, and the birds of the air have nests; but the Son of Man has nowhere to lay His head."[16] Yet He calls Himself greater than Solomon! And He was right. For all the glory of Solomon was as dust and ashes when compared to the divine glory of Jesus. Yet, when we became children of God, this glory became our own! In all truth, therefore, speaking in a spiritual way, we too are much greater than Solomon.

God's Beauty Is Ours

Jesus once said: "See how the lilies of the field grow; they neither toil nor spin, yet I say to you that not even Solomon in all his glory was arrayed like one of these. But if God so clothes the grass of the field, which today is alive and tomorrow is thrown into the oven, how much more you, O you of little faith!"[17] How lovely God made the lilies, the roses, even the little violets by the roadside! Each little flower He has dressed with a glory all its own, which no artist can duplicate and which no one can fully appreciate. And if the beauty and fragrance of simple little flowers can be so delightful, what must be the beauty of our souls when God has filled them with *His own everlasting glory* and given them of *His own divine beauty!* Surely God could never make anything more wonderful than He is Himself. In fact, all created things are but feeble reflections of His divine beauty. Yet it is this very beauty of His that God shares with us when He fills our souls with sanctifying grace and makes us princes and princesses of His heavenly kingdom. We find a certain reflection of this truth in the story of Ezechiel at the beginning of this chapter, where God says of the foundling who had become His queen: "Thou wast perfect through *My beauty which I had put upon thee.*"

---

16 Matthew 8, 20.
17 Matthew 6, 28-30.

If Solomon's earthly kingdom was so beautiful, what must be the glory and beauty of God's heavenly kingdom, which we as His children hope someday to possess! Since all the good things in this world are but poor shadows of heavenly things, we know that there can hardly be any comparison between the glory of earthly kingdoms and the glory of God's kingdom. Consider a beautiful rosebush in full bloom in the glory of the noonday sun. Can we even begin to compare with it, its shadow on the ground? The same is true of an apple tree laden with rosy apples, of a stately cathedral, of a person we dearly love, or of anything else in the world: there is so little resemblance between the shadow and the person or thing that casts the shadow. Yet the difference between earthly and heavenly things is even greater. For the Holy Spirit tells us in the Bible that no human eyes have ever seen, no human ears have ever heard, and no human heart has ever even imagined the wonderful things that God has prepared in heaven for those who love Him.[18]

What words, then, can we use to describe God's kingdom? To what earthly thing can we compare it? None, really. Heaven is truly too beautiful to be described in human words. In fact, the best words or comparisons we can use to describe it do it an injustice, for they bring our idea of heaven down to the level of earthly things. But since we have only our crude earthly words and thoughts to work with, let us begin with them, just as God does when He speaks to us about heaven in the Holy Bible. He tells us, for example, that the very streets of His heavenly city are paved with pure gold instead of stones.[19] In fact,

---

18 See 1 Corinthians 2, 9.

19 "And the street of the city was pure gold, as it were transparent glass." —Apocalypse 21, 21.

everything in it is made of pure gold, clear as glass, and "adorned with every precious stone,"[20] —diamonds and rubies, no doubt, as well as emeralds and many others mentioned by name. The gates themselves are huge pearls[21] mounted in pure gold. And there is no need for lamps in God's heavenly city, because the glory of God fills it and lights it with a light that is clear as crystal and bright as day.[22]

Let us try to imagine a most beautiful heaven made entirely of the finest earthly things we can think of: gold, silver, diamonds, rubies, and every kind of precious stone, beautifully cut and polished. And then let us say to ourselves: Heaven is far more beautiful than that, beautiful beyond my wildest dreams, beautiful as only God's own home can be. For heaven is God's home; and as long as I am in sanctifying grace it is also mine, all mine, forever: for I am His child and He is my loving Father. He is the great heavenly King, and I am His heavenly prince (or princess). How lucky I am to have such a wonderful Father and to be such a privileged person myself—a child of God!

God's Glory Hidden in Our Souls

The thought of heaven is indeed like a beautiful dream, but a dream which will someday surely come true. Since, however, one has to wait so long for this dream to come true, some people get discouraged and forget about it, and

---

20 "And the material of its wall was jasper; but the city itself was pure gold, like pure glass. And the foundations of the wall of the city were adorned with every precious stone." —Apocalypse 21, 18-19.

21 "And the twelve gates were twelve pearls; that is, each gate was of a single pearl." —Apocalypse 21, 21.

22 "Its light was like to a precious stone, as it were a jasper-stone, clear as crystal. . . . And the city has no need of the sun or the moon to shine upon it. For the glory of God lights it up, and the Lamb is the lamp thereof. . . . And night shall be no more, and they shall have no need of light of lamp, or light of sun, for the Lord God will shed light upon them; and they shall reign forever and ever." —Apocalypse 21, 11 and 23; 22, 5.

perhaps live as if God and heaven did not exist—as if they were not His children. We must therefore often renew our thoughts and dreams of heaven, remembering that though we may not actually see the glory of heaven for some time yet, we nevertheless already have it in our own heart. For, as long as we are free from mortal sin, God lives in our heart. And if God lives in our heart, our heart is His home and His heaven.

Mortal Sin Makes Us Children of the Devil

Unfortunately, after becoming children of God, some people commit mortal sins, and this makes them enemies of God and children of the devil. God inspired St. John to write in the Holy Bible: "He who commits sin is of the devil."[23] To commit a mortal sin is to turn away from God, thereby preventing Him from sharing His life with us, and being left, as a tragic consequence, in the immediate danger of eternal damnation. To commit a single mortal sin is, therefore, the worst thing that could ever happen to us in the world; because through mortal sin we lose the new life which we had from God, His wonderful friendship, and our right to His beautiful heaven. And surely these things are more precious by far than even a thousand worlds or a thousand earthly kingdoms.

---

[23] 1 John 3, 8.

from
BUD

to
BLOOM

Chapter II

FROM BUD TO BLOOM

Everybody loves flowers. They have about them a refreshing charm which seems to come from another world. They are like something left over from Paradise, as if planted here by mistake. They bloom for such a short time; then they fade, wither and die—as if they had pined away for a better land they had known. Sometimes their graceful form, lovely colors, and sweet fragrance seem to transport us for a moment into a better world and make us feel like better people.

Perhaps God made the flowers in this drab and gray world to remind us of our true home,[1] a land of eternal bloom, fragrance, and beauty; a land of everlasting song and joy, where the heart never grows tired or old, and where the day is always young.

And of all the flowers that God has made, the rose is the undisputed queen. The rose, especially the fragrant, deeply red rose, is nearly everyone's favorite. We are happy when the first buds appear, because each bud is a promise of a rose bloom. We like to watch the buds slowly grow and swell and open into beautiful blooms. In fact, each rosebud is really a lovely rose neatly rolled up and wrapped into a solid little green bundle. When it opens, the rose appears in all its dainty glory. It is God's tender way of sending us lovely roses fresh and unharmed.

In this world our souls are like the green rosebuds. As long as we live on this earth the divine life which God shares with us is hidden deep in our souls—like a rose in a bud—so that we cannot see or feel it. But after we die, this

---

1 That is, apart from their biological function. God's purposes in the world are more far-reaching than we commonly think.

[13]

life of God will appear in all its wondrous splendor in our souls—like a beautiful, fragrant rose blooming in God's paradise for His honor and glory and our own everlasting delight.

Sometimes we may think that it is too bad that we cannnot see God or feel His tender presence strongly in our hearts. But actually it is a good thing. For if we were to see God for just an instant or feel His presence very strongly in our hearts, we would die of sheer joy or be killed by the splendor of His glory.[2] That is why God once said to Moses: "Thou canst not see My face, for man shall not see Me and live."[3] Many of the saints have at times felt themselves so close to God that they fell into an ecstasy, their bodies often becoming as if dead, while their souls enjoyed the near presence of God. Only God's power kept them from actually dying during that time. It would be a wonderful thing if we could enjoy such an ecstasy just once in our lifetime. But that is reserved only for very good, strong, and holy souls. St. Paul once had such a vision, as he calls it. He says that he became completely unconscious of the world about him and even of his own body and was taken up to "the third heaven," to "paradise," where he "heard secret words" and learned many things from God.[4]

We can scarcely hope to be so privileged in this life. However, if we sincerely try to be good, God does not hide Himself from us altogether, even now. Sometimes we can be aware, just a little, of His gentle presence in our souls; this may most likely happen after we have made a good

---

2 "Reveal Thyself, I cry, though the beauty of Thy presence Kill." —St. John of the Cross, **Works** (London: Burns—Oates, 1943), Vol. II, p. 444.

3 Exodus 33, 20.

4 "If I must boast— . . . I will come to visions and revelations of the Lord. I know a man in Christ who fourteen years ago—whether in the body I do not know, or out of the body I do not know, God knows—such a one was caught up to the third heaven. . . . He was caught up into paradise and heard secret words that man may not repeat." —2 Corinthians 12, 1-4.

confession or have received Jesus very fervently in Holy Communion, or have spent some time in quiet prayer. It is a very pleasant feeling and we know that if it were to increase very much, we would have to die of happiness. So it is really a good thing that God does not let us see Him or feel His presence too strongly. He wants us to believe what He has taught us about heaven and to live a good life; then someday all our beautiful dreams and hopes about heaven will come true.

Chapter III

THE GRAPEVINE OF JESUS

It was just after the Last Supper. Jesus had offered the first Sacrifice of the Mass and had given the Apostles their first Holy Communion. Soon He would be seized and put to death. He was giving them His last instructions as they set out together for the Garden of Olives, where Jesus often went to pray and where He would now be betrayed by Judas. He wanted especially to explain to the Apostles the meaning of the great treasure of sanctifying grace, which made them adopted sons of God and united them so closely with Him that they became spiritually one with Him.

Grace Makes Us One with God

Jesus spoke of this oneness with God when He prayed to the Father after the Last Supper: "That all may be *one,* even as Thou, Father, in Me and I in Thee; that they also may be one in us . . . And the *glory* that Thou hast given Me, *I have given to them, that they may be one, even as we are one: I in them and Thou in Me."*[1] Some time before this, He had said to the Jews, *"I and the Father are one."*[2] And now He tells us that when He gives us a share in His own life and "glory" through sanctifying grace, *we become one with Him.*

The Grapevine Is a Figure of Our Oneness with Christ

It was already night when Jesus began His last walk with His Apostles to His beloved Garden of Olives, about a mile away. The darkness did not trouble them because they knew the way very well, especially after their eyes had become accustomed to the darkness. Perhaps the moon was

1 John 17, 21-23.
2 John 10, 30.

shining too, flooding the countryside with its pale, enchanting light. No doubt it was a pleasant spring evening, though slightly cold. But the Apostles were not paying much attention to the weather, for they were too absorbed in what Jesus was telling them. As they passed along the dark outlines of fig and olive trees, the little group must have paused for a moment now and then as Jesus tried to impress them with some lofty truth about His heavenly kingdom. No doubt they passed a number of grapevines along the way; and Jesus, ever ready to use objects at hand as illustrations for His teachings, must have pointed to one of them as He explained that just as the branches and the stem are but a single vine, so they and He are also one because they and He have the same life of God within themselves.[3] Having received Him into their hearts under the appearances of bread and wine that very evening, the Apostles were well prepared to understand this.

St. John Records the Master's Words

St. John, the Apostle whom Jesus loved more than the others because of his virginity, stayed close to Jesus, listening carefully to His every word. Many years later he wrote those words down in his account of the Gospel. They read as follows: "I am the true vine, and My Father is the vinedresser. Every branch in Me that bears no fruit He will take away; and every branch that bears fruit He will cleanse, that it may bear more fruit. . . . Abide in Me, and I in you. As the branch cannot bear fruit of itself unless it remain on the vine, so neither can you unless you abide

---

[3] It is not certain whether the allegory of the grapevine was spoken in the Cenacle or on the way to Gethsemane. Since the distance between the two places was about a mile, a leisurely walk would have provided ample time for conversation. In the absence of sufficient evidence for either view, there is as much justification for our version as for any other, especially since the words immediately preceding the narrative are, "Arise, let us go from here."

[18]

in Me. I am the vine, you are the branches. He who abides in Me, and I in him, he bears much fruit; for without Me you can do nothing. If anyone does not abide in Me, he shall be cast outside as the branch and wither; and they shall gather them up and cast them into the fire, and they shall burn."[4]

The Apostles, however, were not to be the only branches in the grapevine of Jesus. We, too, are branches of His heavenly vine; and so are all people who have been baptized and have thus become children of God.

Grafting of Trees

Most of us have heard of the process of grafting trees and vines. Grafting is done by taking a small branch from one tree and fixing it into the bark of another tree. If it is done correctly and at the right time of the year, the branch will live and grow and will soon become a part of the tree into which it has been grafted. Sometimes we see an apple tree with as many as five different varieties of apples on it. This means that someone had grafted branches from five different apple trees into the original tree. Grafting is very useful in fruit growing. For example, we may have an apple tree that does not bear good fruit. Instead of chopping it down, we cut its branches off in the early spring, and in their places we graft small branches from a good tree. When the branches become strong enough, they begin to bear good fruit. Whenever we do not like a certain variety of fruit on a tree, we can easily change it by grafting. Most of the fruit trees that we buy for our gardens have already been grafted at the nursery. It is the only sure way the nurserymen have of giving us the exact variety of fruit we want. Grafting, therefore, means the remaking of a tree or

---

4 John 15, 1-2, 4-6.

vine: making a new one out of an old one, a good one out of a bad one.

Spiritual Grafting through Baptism

But trees and vines are not the only things that can be grafted. We often hear of grafts being performed on the human body—skin grafts, bone grafts, and in some cases even grafts of certain vital organs. The same is true, in a different and more lofty sense, of our souls. For, through Baptism, we were grafted, in a spiritual way, into Jesus. We and Jesus then became one, just as the branches and the trunk are but one tree. Jesus then began to live in us, and we in Him. This means that in some mysterious and wonderful way Jesus and we began to live one life together, the very life of God which He has in common with the Father and the Holy Spirit from all eternity.

We Have Two Lives in One

This divine life, however, did not replace our human life but is something extra in our souls which makes our human life much more beautiful. We call it *super*natural life because it is so much better and higher than our natural life. Being grafted into Jesus means, therefore, that our soul has been remade into something better; or, as Jesus says, it has been "reborn." It is like changing a bad tree into a good one by grafting.

Unbaptized Souls

People who have never been baptized (not even with the baptism of blood or desire) are not children of God but "children of wrath," deserving of God's anger because of their sins, which make them slaves of satan.[5] Far from

---

5 "You also, when you were **dead by reason of your offenses and sins,** wherein once you walked according to the fashion of this world, . . . even we, all of us, once led our lives in the desires of our flesh, doing the promptings of our flesh and of our thoughts, and were **by nature children of wrath even as the rest.**" —Ephesians 2, 1-3.

being branches of the heavenly grapevine of Jesus, they are branches of a wild grapevine, nurtured by the devil.[6] Spiritually speaking, the fruit of such souls is often sour and bitter, most displeasing to God.[7]

Good Deeds of Unbaptized Souls

We know from everyday experience that people who are not baptized can do many good deeds. But such good deeds do not deserve a heavenly reward; though God often does reward them with earthly blessings or with the grace of conversion. However, since people are strongly inclined to evil, on account of original sin, and since unbaptized persons lack many of God's graces, it is very difficult for them to avoid mortal sin. That is why, when left without the true religion, pagan peoples often fall to the lowest depths of wickedness.

Examples from History

In the days of Noe, people became so bad that in a great flood God destroyed all of them except Noe and his family.[8] In the days of Lot, God destroyed the cities of Sodom and Gomorrha because the sins of the people were so great that they cried to heaven for vengeance. Yet, according to His promise, God would have spared Sodom if He could have found just ten good people in it.[9]

We have all heard of the sinful ways of pagan Rome. One of the favorite pastimes of the Romans—as popular

---

6 "And He [God] looked that it should bring forth grapes, and it brought forth wild grapes." —Isaias 5, 2.
"He who commits sin is of the devil." —1 John 3, 8.
"The father from whom you are is the devil." —John 8, 44.

7 "Their grapes are grapes of gall, and their clusters most bitter. Their wine is the gall of dragons, and the venom of asps, which is incurable." —Deuteronomy 32, 32-33.

8 Genesis, chapters 6-8.

9 Genesis, chapters 18-19, especially 18, 32.

with them as baseball with Americans—was to go to the arena to see people devoured by beasts, killed with swords, or burned alive. It took Christianity a long time to free the Romans from this vice. And in our own country, letters from the early missionaries to the American Indians describe a shocking immorality and superstition on the part of those pagan peoples.

When godless people begin to follow their evil inclinations they often become so bad that nothing seems too wicked for them to do. Some of them even stoop so low as to offer human beings in sacrifice to devils! And who has forgotten the terrible crimes against human beings committed in our own times by godless Nazis and Communists! Our Christian conscience is stunned when we read of some of these misdeeds, and we thank God that through Baptism and our holy Faith we have been freed from the cruel tyranny and slavery of satan.

God's Grapevine in Pictures

In His many sermons to the people, Jesus liked to use as examples and illustrations the various things He saw during His missionary journeys. For instance, when the Apostles made the miraculous catch of fish, He told them that in the same way they would soon be catching souls for God. This method of teaching made it easier for the people to understand Him.

If we could have a grapevine before us the way Jesus probably did when explaining His lesson on the mystery of God's life in us, we could understand it much better too. But since we have no real grapevine to look at, let us content ourselves with some drawings while using our imagination.

In the first drawing (Figure 1) we see a grapevine. It has four branches covered with leaves and grapes.[10] Jesus compared Himself to the main parts of this vine, the roots

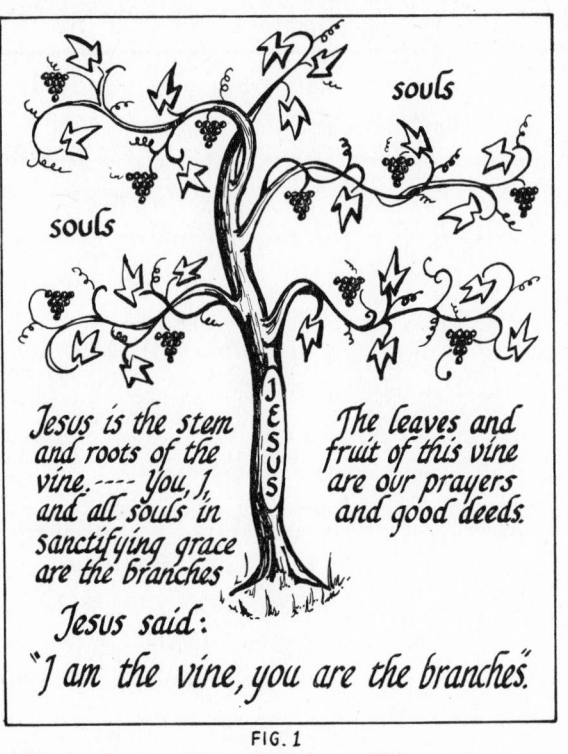

souls

souls

Jesus is the stem and roots of the vine.---- You, I, and all souls in sanctifying grace are the branches

The leaves and fruit of this vine are our prayers and good deeds.

Jesus said:

"I am the vine, you are the branches."

FIG. 1

and the stem, and us to the branches. The stem and the branches a r e not the same thing, but they do form a single v i n e, and have one and the same life. In much the same way, we b e c a m e one with Jesus t h r o u g h B a p t i s m . Without losing any of o u r natural l i f e ,

and without changing into Him, we came to possess His divine life in our souls. Notice that we said "His *divine* life," and not "His human life." For Jesus also has a human life and nature like ours, and, besides this, the divine life which He has always had as God. We have His human life in us only when we receive Holy Communion (until the sacred species dissolve in our stomachs); but His divine life

10 Cultivated grapevines are often trained to have four fruit-bearing branches running in two directions on horizontal wires.

continues to stay in our souls as long as we are free from mortal sin. And it is this divine life, remaining permanently in our souls, that makes us His children, beautiful and glorious in His sight, and most pleasing to Him.

Life versus Death

We often see dead branches on trees and shrubs but never pay much attention to them. But the next time we see a dead branch on a tree let us look at it very carefully and compare it with a live one. What a difference! Like that between night and day, to use the familiar expression. And what makes this difference? It is *life*. The one has life, and the other does not. The same is true of a human soul. Without the life of God, a soul is like a dead branch; with the life of God, it is like a live one.

The Fruit of a Soul in Sanctifying Grace

Every good grapevine bears good fruit in abundance. The spiritual grapevine of Jesus, in which He is the root and stem, and we the branches, must also bear good spiritual fruit. This fruit is our prayers and good deeds. If we are free from mortal sin, our prayers and good deeds are pleasing to God, and He will reward us in heaven. That is what Jesus meant when He said, "He who abides in Me, and I in him, he bears much fruit."[11]

Perhaps there is a grapevine or a fruit tree in our yard or garden. If so, we know how good it feels to see that vine or tree heavily laden with luscious, colorful fruit, so that the branches bend to the very ground. That is how God feels when a soul is free from mortal sin and lives a good

11 John 15, 5.

life, full of good deeds done for God and our fellow man. Humanly speaking, it really makes His heart glad; and the reward He prepares for such a soul in heaven is too great for our minds to understand in this world.[12]

Mortal Sin Means the Loss of Supernatural Life

The two branches which have been cut off the vine are like two souls in mortal sin ---- they are cut off from Jesus.

JESUS

Branches separated from the vine soon wilt and die. Souls separated from Jesus are spiritually dead.
The fruit of dead branches is ruined. The prayers and good deeds of people in mortal sin are lost — until they go to Confession.

FIG. 2

Grapes grow on the branches of a vine, but the branches grow on the stem. If a branch is severed from the stem, it soon wilts and dies, along with its leaves, tendrils and fruit. And new fruit can no longer grow on it. Jesus said, "If anyone does not abide in Me, he shall be cast outside as the branch

---

12 "Rejoice and exult, because your reward is great in heaven." —Matthew 5, 12.

"Eye has not seen nor ear heard, nor has it entered into the heart of man, what things God has prepared for those who love Him." —1 Corinthians 2, 9.

and wither."[13] In Figure 2, we see that the two lower branches of our grapevine have been cut off and are lying on the ground, wilted and dying—like two souls separated from God through mortal sin.

Jesus also said: "As the branch cannot bear fruit of itself unless it remain on the vine, so neither can you unless you abide in Me."[14] This means that we cannot please God or do good deeds for heaven unless we are united with Him through sanctifying grace. If we are cut away from Him through mortal sin, His life disappears from our souls and we become like dead branches. We cannot then bear any fruit for heaven, because if we are spiritually dead our prayers and good deeds have no supernatural worth.

Penance Means a Return of Supernatural Life

Jesus knew that some people would commit mortal sins after Baptism and would thus be separated from Him, becoming like dead branches which cannot bear fruit. But He also knew that many sinners would later be sorry for their sins and would want to come back to Him. So, in His great goodness and love for us, He gave us a means of having our sins forgiven and of regaining His life in our souls. He gave us the Sacrament of Penance—or Confession, as we often call it—so that we can be united with Him again, just as a branch can be grafted back into a vine.

---

13 John 15, 6.
14 John 15, 4.

This branch was grafted back into the vine. It lives and yields fruit—like a soul that has gone to Confession, and is again alive with the life of Jesus.

This branch was not grafted back into the vine. It has withered and died—like a soul that has died in mortal sin.

JESUS

The merits of souls that die in mortal sin are lost—like fruit on dead branches.

(Actually, grafting is done in the spring before the leaves appear. Grafting a fruiting vine, as here illustrated would scarcely be possible.)

FIG. 3

In Figure 3 we see that one of the severed branches has been grafted back into the vine. It lives and bears fruit. The other was not grafted back and has died. The same is true of a human soul that has committed a mortal sin. If it returns to Jesus through a good Confession (o r perfect contrition) it becomes one with Him again, and He makes it live with His life once more and bear fruit for heaven. But if the soul is not sorry for its sins and does not return to Jesus, but leaves this world in mortal sin, it is lost forever with all the merits of its prayers and good deeds.

What a wonderful sacrament Penance is! If Jesus had not given us this holy sacrament, we would have no sure and safe way of becoming His friends again, of being united with Him again and of getting His life back into our souls.

And if we committed even one mortal sin, we might be lost forever.

Perfect Contrition

A sinner could indeed make an act of perfect contrition and so regain God's grace and friendship. But how can anyone ever be *sure* that his contrition is perfect? Perfect contrition presupposes perfect love of God. It means that we detest sin more than any other evil in the world because it offends God, whom we love with our whole heart. It may, therefore, be quite easy for a good person, who sincerely loves God above all things, to make an act of perfect contrition. But, for a big sinner, especially one who has been resisting God's graces and living in sin for some time, it might be quite difficult to suddenly begin to love God perfectly and to have perfect sorrow for his sins. But even if God, in His goodness, gave the sinner the grace to make an act of perfect sorrow, he would have no way of definitely knowing that he had it. Such a poor sinner might either be falsely persuading himself that he had perfect sorrow, or he might be needlessly anxious and worried, even to the point of despair. When one receives the Sacrament of Penance, however, even with imperfect contrition and with ordinary diligence, one can be reasonably sure that one's sins are forgiven, because of Christ's promise. The Sacrament of Penance is, therefore, a much easier, safer and surer way of having our sins forgiven. (Moreover, since Christ has given us the Sacrament of Penance, we are obliged to confess all our mortal sins, even if we should be sure of having perfect contrition.)

Penance is a "Lifesaver"

How thankful to God should we be then, for this sacrament! But maybe, instead of being grateful to God, some of us consider this sacrament a burden. Confession may not be easy or pleasant, because we do not like to admit that we did wrong; but it is the sure and safe way which Christ gave us of becoming a part of His spiritual grapevine again. Difficult though it may seem at times, Confession is certainly a great blessing of God, a real "lifesaver," for it saves us from everlasting death in hell. Confession makes us feel much better and happier too by giving us peace of mind. Somebody once said, "Before Confession I feel heavy as lead, but after Confession I feel light as a bird." Everybody who makes a good and sincere Confession feels that way. How sad that very many people receive this sacrament so seldom! Every good Catholic should confess his sins frequently. But if one has the misfortune to commit a serious sin, one should try to make an act of perfect contrition at once and go to Confession as soon as possible to avoid the awful risk of dying in sin. And we should always receive this sacrament with faith and sincerity, remembering the words of Jesus to His Apostles and to all of His priests: "Receive the Holy Spirit; whose sins you shall forgive, they are forgiven them; and whose sins you shall retain, they are retained."[15]

Holy Communion Is the Heavenly Food of the Soul

Like all living things, a grapevine needs food and drink in order to live. Its food and drink are a substance which we call sap. There are really two kinds of sap in the vine, and each is of equal importance in its life. If either stops flowing, the vine dies. The first kind of sap supplies the vine with the water and minerals it needs. It flows up through the vine from the roots to the leaves. The second kind is produced by the vine itself and flows from the leaves downward through the whole vine. This latter sap begins

---

15 John 20, 22-23.

its existence in the leaves of the vine as a simple mixture of starch and water. The starch itself is produced in the leaves from water and carbon dioxide, with the help of sunlight. The carbon dioxide is absorbed by the leaves from the air. As the sap slowly flows down through the various parts of the vine, it is digested and changed by chemical action into the sugars, proteins, vitamins and other compounds which the vine needs to live and grow. The vine uses these to form the tiny cells or living "building-blocks" which it adds to its own substance as it grows and with which it builds for us its clusters of juicy grapes.

This, in short, is the story of the sap in a grapevine, from the time its first elements enter the roots and the leaves to the time they become a part of the living vine or its fruit. It is a beautiful story, full of mysteries. Indeed, these are the secrets of life itself, upon which all life in the world depends; and which man, with all his earnest searching, has not been able to grasp or imitate—perhaps never shall.

We know that no comparison is perfect, especially if one tries to compare sublime spiritual truths to earthly things. And the more sublime the spiritual truth, the more difficult it is to compare it to something earthly. The reader will therefore excuse any defects in our comparison as we presume to liken the wonderful earthly mystery of sap in the grapevine to the infinitely more wondrous heavenly mystery of Holy Communion, by which the human soul is nourished with the very substance of the incarnate Son of God.

We have seen how the vine changes the earthly elements of water, minerals, air and light into sap, which finally becomes a part of the very substance of the vine, making it grow and bear fruit. So it is, if we may make the comparison, with Holy Communion. Jesus changes the earthly elements of bread and wine into His own Body and **Blood**, so that we, His branches, may be nourished with His own substance. But Jesus is God as well as man. And as God He has a divine substance, a divine life and nature. This He also shares with us in a marvelous way in Holy Communion. Like the sap of life in a grapevine, the divine food of Holy Communion flows spiritually through our soul, nourishing, strengthening, and increasing in it the divine life which we have from God, making it grow, thrive, and bear abundant fruit for heaven.

Holy Communion is as necessary for the supernatural life and vigor of our souls as an abundance of sap is for the life and vigorous growth of a grapevine. A vine cannot live without sap: neither can our soul have divine life unless it be nourished with the divine food and drink of the Body and Blood of Jesus. That is why Jesus said: "Amen, amen, I say to you, unless you eat the flesh of the Son of Man, and drink His blood, you shall not have life in you."[16]

Spiritual Communion

One might object that our comparison is not true, because in every age there are good people, even saints, who grow in grace and holiness, although they are unable to receive Holy Communion often; a vine could not thrive thus without sap. We answer that God keeps the grapevine alive through the long months and killing frosts of winter, even though no sap flows through it. Certainly, He would not do less for souls that love Him. Holy Communion is a wonderful channel of grace given us by God. But God can and often does give His graces through other channels, especially if the regular ones cannot be used. Unable to feed their souls with the Bread of Live, devout souls often

---

16 John 6, 54.

hunger for God with a great longing. And this hunger is for them a continuous spiritual Communion, rich in graces and blessings. We should imitate them in this, always yearning for closer union with Jesus; but we should also receive the Sacrament itself as often as we can. For if Holy Communion were not so important in our supernatural life, Christ would not have called it "the Bread of Life," nor would He have warned us that its absence in our spiritual diet means spiritual death.

Frequent Holy Communion Means a Vigorous Spiritual Life

Not all branches in a grapevine grow equally well. Some are weak and small and produce little fruit; others are very vigorous and produce much fruit. This is due to the fact that, because of their position in the vine, some branches receive more sap than others. The same is true of our souls. If we receive Holy Communion often, we become very strong spiritually. And when we are spiritually strong, we not only bear more fruit of good deeds for heaven but we are also able to resist more firmly the temptations to mortal sin which could make us die spiritually. A vigorous branch can resist disease more easily than an under-nourished one. In the same way, a soul that is rich in grace through close union with Christ can resist temptations to every kind of sin more easily than one which is spiritually weak through lack of grace.

Spiritual Pruning

In His story of the grapevine, Jesus also said, "Every branch that bears fruit He [the Father] will cleanse, that it may bear more fruit."[17] To cleanse a branch means, in our way of speaking here, to prune it. And by pruning we mean cutting away certain useless parts of a branch which

---

17 John 15, 2.

only interfere with its fruit-bearing, or which, if allowed to grow, would overwork the vine. Every fruit grower knows that in order to get a good crop of fruit he must prune his trees correctly and often severely. The same is true, Jesus says, of His spiritual grapevine. The branches, which are human souls, must be pruned or "cleansed," often severely, in order to bear abundant fruit. God does this by sending trials and sufferings to the souls He wants to make holy. We read in the Holy Bible, "Whom the Lord loveth, He chastiseth."[18] This means that God often sends the greatest sufferings to persons whom He loves most. Jesus, His own Son, suffered most of all. And all God's saints have to suffer in proportion to their holiness. In fact, it is difficult to imagine holiness without suffering.

Jesus once said, "If anyone wishes to come after Me, let him deny himself, and take up his cross, and follow Me."[19] Good Christians not only cheerfully accept sufferings sent them by God, but even impose some on themselves by doing penance, such as fasting, giving alms to the needy, and denying themselves in many little ways. Their sufferings and penances not only help to make them pure and holy, but are also some of the good fruit which they bear for heaven, because in heaven they shall be richly rewarded for the sufferings they endured for love of God.

After Death

Dead branches are of little use to anyone. They are usually burned as rubbish. The same is true of people who die as enemies of God, in mortal sin. They are of no use to anybody; they are burned forever in hell. Jesus said, "If anyone does not abide in Me, he shall be cast outside

---

18 Proverbs 3, 12.
19 Matthew 16, 24.

as the branch and wither; and they shall gather them up and cast them into the fire, and they shall burn."[20] But all the good people who were faithful branches of the spiritual grapevine of Jesus, alive and vigorous with His divine life, and who bore much fruit of prayer, penance and good deeds, will enjoy forever with Jesus the riches, happiness and glory of His heavenly kingdom.

---

[20] John 15, 6.

"Jesus then took the loaves, and when He had given thanks, distributed them to those reclining; and likewise the fishes, as much as they wished."

JOHN 6, 11.

Chapter IV

THE LIVING BREAD OF JESUS

We read in the Gospels how Jesus spent the last years of His life going about all the towns and villages of His country doing good to all. He spoke of His heavenly kingdom and taught people how to live in order to become worthy of this kingdom. He cured the sick, even raised the dead, and worked countless other miracles. Soon everybody was talking about Him and great crowds followed Him wherever He went, listening to His teachings and asking for cures and favors.[1] This kept Jesus and the Apostles so busy that they had little time to rest or even to take food.[2]

Jesus Multiplies Bread and Fishes[3]

One day Jesus decided to take His Apostles by boat to a lonely place across the Sea of Galilee to give them a chance to take a rest, away from the crowds. But somehow the people found out where they were going, and set out for the place on foot, announcing the news to everybody they met on the way. When Jesus and the Apostles finally landed at their destination, a great crowd was already there waiting for them. As usual, Jesus began to teach and to cure the sick. Toward evening, the Apostles suggested that Jesus send the people away to find food for themselves and a place to sleep. But Jesus felt sorry for them, for He knew that they were very hungry; many of them had come from afar and had been following Him for some time. He decided to feed them there in the wilderness. But where could they buy enough food for so many? Philip estimated that a

---

1 See Matthew 4, 23-24; 9, 35; John 6, 2.
2 Mark 6, 31.
3 For this story see John 6, 1-15; Mark 6, 30-44; Matthew 14, 13-21; Luke 9, 10-17.

workingman's wages for two hundred days could scarcely buy enough bread to give each one a little. Jesus asked the Apostles to find out whether anyone in the crowd had any food. A hurried search yielded only five loaves of barley bread and two fishes, the jealously guarded property of a small boy. Since the loaves and fishes were quite small, this would have been enough to feed only about two or three hungry men.[4]

The Apostles thought that Jesus would surely change His mind about trying to feed the huge crowd, and would send them home. On the contrary, He seemed more determined than ever. He bade the Apostles to make the people recline on the soft spring grass in groups of fifties and hundreds like so many patches of flowers on a lawn. Then He took the bread and fishes into His hands, and looking up into heaven, He prayed over them and blessed them and began to divide them into portions for the disciples to give to the people.

We can suppose that the boy had not been very willing at first to part with his bread and fishes. But now his eyes opened wide with wonder, for the bread and fishes began to multiply miraculously in the hands of Jesus. The Apostles filled their baskets and, walking among the groups of people, gave to all as much as they could eat. Again and again they returned to Jesus and carried away basket after basket of the bread and fishes to the hungry crowd, until all had been satisfied. There were about five thousand men there, not counting the numerous women and children. And when all had eaten as much as they wanted, there were still twelve baskets of pieces left over. And no doubt the young boy had more provisions in his basket after the meal was over than

_____
4 See Luke 11, 5-8.

[38]

before it began. Nor could he ever forget how so little had become so very much before his very eyes.

When the people had seen this great miracle, they said, "This is indeed the Prophet who is to come into the world."[5] They wanted to take Him by force and make Him their king. But Jesus slipped away and went up a mountain alone to pray. He always did that. After teaching and helping people all day, He would go in the evening to a quiet place and pray for a long time, sometimes even all night, to His Father.

Jesus Promises To Give Us Living Bread

During the night Jesus crossed the stormy Sea of Galilee by walking on the waves and rejoined His Apostles, who had gone before Him in their boat. The next day, after much searching, the crowd finally crossed the lake in boats and found Jesus at Capharnaum. We might think that Jesus would be very happy to see how eagerly the crowd sought Him. On the contrary, He scolded them, for He knew that their chief interest in seeking Him was just another free meal. He said: "Amen, amen, I say to you, you seek Me, not because you have seen signs, but because you have eaten of the loaves and have been filled. Do not labor for the food that perishes, but for that which endures unto life everlasting, which the Son of Man will give you."[6]

The people did not understand what Jesus meant by food which endures unto life everlasting. Recalling, however, how, long ago, at the time of Moses, God had fed the Hebrews in the desert with a miraculous food called manna,[7] they thought that perhaps Jesus was going to give them a similar, miraculous bread from heaven. Imagine having a

---

5 John 6, 14.
6 John 6, 26-27.
7 See Exodus 16, 31-35.

miraculous loaf of bread which would keep growing as fast as one could eat it! Their minds must have been full of expectation and suspense as Jesus continued: "Amen, amen, I say to you, Moses did not give you the bread from heaven, but My Father gives you the true bread from heaven. For the bread of God is that which comes down from heaven and gives life to the world."[8] They guessed that Jesus intended to give them something even better than the miraculous manna, and they called out, "Lord, give us always this bread."[9]

Jesus Himself Is Our Living Bread from Heaven

Jesus answered, "I am the bread of life."[10] The people did not understand what He meant. They looked at one another and began to murmur about Him. What is He talking about, they wondered. *He* is the bread that came down from heaven! Is He joking? But Jesus calmly continued: "I am the bread of life. Your fathers ate the manna in the desert, and have died. This is the bread that comes down from heaven, so that if anyone eat of it he will not die. I am the *living bread* that has come down from heaven. If anyone eat of this bread he shall live forever; and the bread that I will give is My flesh for the life of the world."[11]

The Jews Misunderstand Him

At these words the people became restless and noisy, arguing with one another and saying, "How can this man give us His flesh to eat?"[12] They imagined that Jesus meant that He was going to cut His body into slices and thus give them His flesh to eat. They stared at Him, many with

8 John 6, 32-33.
9 John 6, 34.
10 John 6, 35.
11 John 6, 48-52.
12 John 6, 53.

anger and disgust, ready to call Him a madman.[13] Who ever heard, they murmered, of a man giving away his own flesh to be eaten? Why, that would be cannibalism!

His Flesh and Blood Are To Be Our Living Food and Drink

Jesus did not even try to correct the mistaken notions of the crowd. He knew that people of good will would believe Him even if they did not understand. But the wicked would not believe even if they understood. So He calmly looked at the disturbed crowd before Him and said slowly and with great tenderness and solemnity: "Amen, amen, I say to you, unless you eat the flesh of the Son of Man, and drink His blood, you shall not have life in you. He who eats My flesh and drinks My blood has life everlasting and I will raise him up on the last day. For My flesh is food indeed, and My blood is drink indeed. He who eats My flesh, and drinks My blood, abides in Me and I in him. As the *living Father* has sent Me, and as *I live* because of the Father, so he who eats Me, he also shall *live* because of Me. This is the bread that has come down from heaven; not as your fathers ate the manna, and died. He who eats this bread shall live forever."[14]

Some of His Friends Leave Him

We who understand these words know that they are among the most beautiful ever spoken by Jesus. But many of the people who heard them then did not think so. In fact, many of Jesus' own disciples, His especially chosen friends, said, "This is a hard saying. Who can listen to it?"[15] And they left Jesus and no longer followed Him or listened to Him.

---

13 In another place we read: "Many of them were saying, 'He has a devil and is mad.'" —John 10, 20.

14 John 6, 54-59.

15 John 6, 61.

[41]

A whole year went by and many of the people had almost forgotten what Jesus had said about giving them living bread from heaven. Perhaps His own Apostles only vaguely remembered His words. But at the Last Supper, the night before Jesus died, those memorable words came back to their minds with all their sublime meaning; for it was then that Jesus fulfilled His promise. After the supper, with the eyes of the Apostles fixed intently upon Him, Jesus took some unleavened bread into His hands, raised His eyes to heaven and prayed fervently to His Father as He blessed it. A deep silence fell over the Apostles as they recalled how Jesus had blessed and broken the bread in the desert and how it had multiplied so that thousands had more than enough to eat. Was He going to repeat that miracle now? Maybe He would give them a miraculous bread which would never be used up no matter how much they ate of it. Knowing His great power over all things, they knew that anything could happen. Full of expectation, they watched. Jesus' face was radiant and His eyes glistened as never before. For three long years they had been with Him, sharing in all His arduous journeys and labors, His joys and His sorrows. They had studied His face when He wept and when He rejoiced, when He was angry and when He was meek. They had seen the majesty in His face when He worked His greatest miracles. But never before had they seen Him quite like this. Never before had He seemed so kind and good, so majestic, so noble; so gentle, yet so strong; so joyful, yet so sad. This, they sensed, would be the greatest miracle of them all, the crowning work of His life. But what would it be? Jesus continued His prayer for a few breathless moments and then began to devoutly break the bread and to give the morsels to His Apostles, saying with unspeakable tenderness, "Take and eat; this is My Body."[16]

Bread—His body! Awe-struck though they were, they suddenly remembered how He had said: "The bread that I will give is My flesh for the life of the world." Not understanding, yet believing, they received the precious morsels from the hands of Him whom they had come to believe was the Son of God.[17] And as they did so, they became aware of the sublime meaning of those words of Jesus, so disturbing to many a year before: "He who eats My flesh, and drinks My blood, abides in Me and I in him." Till now they had been conscious of the presence of Jesus only outside themselves. Now they became conscious of His presence within their own minds and hearts. It was a completely new experience in their lives. Jesus had said, "If anyone eat of this bread he shall live forever." How could it be otherwise, with their souls thus immersed in the living God?

The Cup of Living Wine

Jesus had also promised to give them His blood to drink. So now He took a chalice of wine, blessed it and gave it to them to drink, saying, "All of you drink of this; for this is My blood."[18] And as each drank the priceless drops of "living wine" and fell into a little ecstasy of thanksgiving, each one now, at last, understood so well what Jesus meant when He said, "My flesh is food indeed, and My blood is drink indeed." Under the appearances of earthly food and drink—bread and wine—they now experienced in their hearts, as if in a tangible manner, the great mystery of God sharing His life with them, His life becoming their own. For the first time in the history of the world, man ate "true

---

16 Matthew 26, 26.

17 "Simon Peter answered and said, 'Thou art the Christ, the Son of the living God.'" —Matthew 16, 16.

18 Matthew 26, 28.

bread from heaven" and nourished his soul with the substance of God.

For All Mankind

Happily for us, the Apostles were not to be the only ones so fortunate. Christ had promised to give His flesh and blood as food and drink to everybody. And He fulfilled this promise at the Last Supper when He commanded His Apostles, "Do this in remembrance of Me,"[19] thus giving to them and to their successors to the end of time the power to give to all mankind what He had given them—living food and drink from heaven.

Christ's Living Bread Necessary for Our Spiritual Health

In His conversation with Nicodemus one night, Jesus said: "God so loved the world that He gave His only-begotten Son, that those who believe in Him may not perish, but may have life everlasting."[20] This "life everlasting," as we have seen in preceding chapters, begins for us already here in this world through the gift of sanctifying grace, which makes our souls—as much as this is possible—like God, by giving us a share in His own divine life and nature, making us thereby in all truth His children, with all the rights, honors, and privileges belonging to such a noble state.

But, unfortunately, we can lose this priceless dignity through a single mortal sin, thus bringing to naught in our souls the fruit of Christ's labors and bitter Passion. Knowing our weakness and the many temptations which constantly beset us in this life, Jesus chose to let us share in His own strength by making Himself the food of our souls. For He knew that if we nourished our souls constantly with His substance, His life would become firmly and deeply rooted

---

19 1 Corinthians 11, 24.
20 John 3, 16.

[44]

in our souls and we would not be easily overcome by the temptations of the flesh, the world, and the devil.

We all know, even from experience, that if a person does not eat enough good food regularly, he becomes thin and weak, then sick, and finally he may even die. The same is no less true of the supernatural life of our souls. If we do not eat the Living Bread of Holy Communion regularly, our souls become spiritually weak, then sick, and finally, in a spiritual way, they may die through mortal sin. That is what Jesus meant when He said: "Unless you eat the flesh of the Son of Man, and drink His blood, you shall not have life in you."

The Difference between Ordinary Bread and Christ's Living Bread

We must not imagine, however, that Holy Communion nourishes our souls in exactly the same way that earthly food nourishes our bodies. The difference between the two is, quite literally, as great as that between heaven and earth: for Holy Communion is truly a bit of heaven, while earthly food, like our own bodies, is just a bit of earthly dust. Ordinary food does indeed nourish our bodies, but it does not give us life, for it has no life to give—it is lifeless, dead. In fact, in a certain sense, our bodies give life to the food we eat, inasmuch as some of the food becomes a part of our living bodies. Holy Communion, on the contrary, is "Living Bread," because it is the living God-Man Himself who comes into our souls under the appearances of earthly bread. And precisely because He is *Living Bread,* He is able to infuse His "life everlasting" into our souls. When we partake of this Living Bread, we do not change it into our own substance, as we do with earthly food: rather, it changes us, making our souls ever more like God. And, whereas earthly food increases our natural energy and strength of body, the

Living Bread of Holy Communion increases God's strength in our soul, endowing it with supernatural vigor and energy.

God's Most Wonderful Sacrament

Of all the wonderful sacraments that God has given us, His Living Bread is the most excellent, because in Holy Communion God gives us Himself. And He gives us Himself in order to make us ever more like Himself in supernatural goodness, beauty, strength, wisdom and all the other wonderful gifts which are the happy lot of His children. God does not need outside food to sustain Him, for He is Life itself. And, since we are His adopted children, His heavenly princes and princesses, it has pleased Him to feed us already here on earth with that same Life, with food worthy of our dignity—heavenly bread indeed!

"Everyone who drinks of this water will thirst again. He, however, who drinks of the water that I will give him shall never thirst; but the water that I will give him shall become in him a fountain of water springing up unto life everlasting."

JOHN 4, 13-14

Chapter V

THE LIVING WATER OF JESUS

Water As Precious As Life

Palestine becomes very hot and dry in the summertime, when no rain falls for about five months, and hot, scorching winds blow in from the Arabian desert. This makes life hard for the people. They often suffer from thirst and have to drink much water to survive the fierce heat. Water is as important and as precious to them as life itself, for without it they would soon die. This, of course, is true of all people in all climates, but it is in the hot climates especially that people realize the importance of water.

Jacob's Well

In order to have enough water to live, the people in Palestine must dig deep wells in the ground. Water can usually be found in the earth if one digs deep enough and in the right place. In fact, well-diggers often strike an underground stream between layers of rock and their well thus becomes a precious spring, from which clean, cool water flows continually. Many centuries before Christ was born, the Patriarch Jacob dug such a well near the foot of Mount Garizim, in the central portion of Palestine known to us as Samaria. The well is still in use today and is called Jacob's Well. It is nearly one hundred feet deep and seven and one-half feet in diameter and is fed by a vigorous spring, probably an underground rivulet draining the nearby mountain.

Jesus at Jacob's Well

One day, as Jesus was walking with His disciples through Samaria, they came to Jacob's Well. It was high noon and very hot. As Jesus was quite tired from His long walk in the blazing sun, He sat down by the well to rest. The disciples, in the meantime, went to a nearby town to buy some food. Jesus must have been very thirsty; but the well was deep and He had nothing to reach the water with. He knew, however, that someone would come to the well for water and would give Him a drink. So He waited patiently while resting His tired feet.

The Samaritan Woman

Soon He saw a Samaritan woman coming to the well with a water jar on her head. Being God as well as man, Jesus knew all the secrets of her heart. He knew that she was living a sinful life because she was living with a man who was not her husband according to the law of God. Jesus knew that her soul was dead in sin and that she was an unhappy woman. But He also knew that she had a good heart and could be moved to give up her sinful union and to lead a holy life.

She Draws Water

As she approached the well, the woman looked up and saw Jesus. She did not know who He was, but she noticed from His clothing and appearance that He was not a Samaritan but a Jew. Now the Samaritans and Jews were unfriendly toward one another for religious, racial and other reasons. The Samaritan woman was somewhat disturbed at the thought of having to draw water in the company of this lone Jewish stranger. But what could she do? She had to have water. So she continued on her way to the well, ignoring Jesus as she came. Perhaps she expected Him to turn the other way as she approached, to show His dislike for a Samaritan. She was accustomed to such treatment. But Jesus did nothing of the kind. She noticed through the corner of her eye that He not only was not snubbing her, but was actually watching her as she lowered her water jar on a rope to the cool depths far below. She became somewhat self-conscious and uneasy, perhaps even wishing that He would turn His face away. But there He sat, so calm and relaxed, studying her every move as she slowly began the task of lifting her heavy burden of cool, life-giving water to the surface. Breathing hard from the exertion, she finally set the dripping water jar on the low wall surrounding the well and hastily prepared to lift it to her head to carry it away.

"Give Me To Drink"

But this stranger by the well! Who is He? And what does He want? She knew that He had walked a long way, for His feet, sandals and the bottom of His once-white tunic were brown with the dust of the parched country roads. Her feminine curiosity got the better of her and she cast a furtive glance at His face as she turned to leave. Then she stopped in her tracks, and her gaze returned to His kindly face, for Jesus had greeted her with a friendly smile and was gently asking, "Give me to drink."[1] Her glance became a surprised stare, for she well knew that to share her water with Him meant friendship and hospitality, something very rare between members of the two unfriendly nations. After a moment of hesitation, she answered, "How is it that Thou, although Thou art a Jew, dost ask drink of me, who am a Samaritan woman?"[2]

He Has "Living Water"

Jesus did not even try to explain Himself, but only answered, "If thou didst know the gift of God, and who it is who says to thee, 'Give me to drink,' thou, perhaps,

---

[1] John 4, 8.
[2] John 4, 9.

wouldst have asked of Him, and He would have given thee *living water.*"[3] The woman did not understand what Jesus meant by "living water." She thought He meant water from a spring, the pure, clear kind that bubbles out of the earth and by its motion appears to be alive. That is what people in Palestine understood by "living water," in opposition to the stagnant water of their many cisterns. In fact, the water from Jacob's Well was that kind of living water, for its source, as we have already mentioned, was a deep spring.

"Whence Hast Thou Living Water?"

The woman was puzzled. If Jesus had living water to give her, why was He asking her for some of hers? In a confused tone of voice she answered, "Sir, Thou hast nothing to draw with, and the well is deep. Whence then has Thou living water?"[4] Yet she understood that Jesus was hinting that He had better water to give her than the water from Jacob's Well, and that He was someone greater than an ordinary person; so she continued, "Art Thou greater than our father Jacob who gave us the well, and drank from it, himself, and his sons, and his flocks?"[5]

Christ's "Living Water" Foretold by the Prophets

Being a Samaritan, the woman did not know, as the Jews did, that the holy prophets had foretold that the Saviour of the world would give mankind "living water" to drink. Thus, the prophet Zachary had said, "And it shall come to pass in that day that *living waters* shall go out from Jerusalem."[6] And the prophet Isaias had written, "You shall draw waters with joy out of the Saviour's fountains.'"[7]

---

3 John 4, 10.
4 John 4, 11.
5 John 4, 12.
6 Zachary 14, 8.
7 Isaias 12, 3.

By telling the woman that He could give her "living water," Jesus was really telling her that He was the promised Saviour of the world; but she did not understand.

"Give Me This Water"

After a few draughts of the cool, refreshing drink which the woman had given Him, Jesus continued, "Everyone who drinks of this water will thirst again. He, however, who drinks of the water that I will give him shall never thirst; but the water that I will give him shall become in him a fountain of water, springing up unto life everlasting."[8] The woman reflected, wondering in her heart how any water could so quench her thirst that she would never be thirsty again. If someone else had said those words, she would have laughed at him; but this stranger, Jesus, had already won her trust and respect. There was a certain majesty, power and dignity about Him which reached to the very bottom of her soul. He spoke so confidently and sincerely of that "living water" which would take away a person's thirst forever. She began to suspect that His words had some higher meaning. Yet, in the circumstances, she preferred, at least for the moment, not to betray her thoughts, but to cling to the idea of earthly water. So she answered, "Sir, give me this water that I may not thirst, or come here to draw."[9]

"Living Water" Means Sanctifying Grace

Some time later, Jesus spoke again of His "living water." But this time it was before a big crowd in the temple at Jerusalem. St. John the Evangelist tells us that Jesus stood in the temple and cried out, saying, "If anyone thirst, let him come to Me and drink. He who believes in Me, as the Scripture says, 'From within him there shall flow *rivers* of

8 John 4, 13-14.
9 John 4, 15.

living water.' "[10] And St. John hastens to explain that by "rivers of living water" Jesus meant the Spirit whom those who believed were one day to receive. This, in turn, means not only the Person of the Holy Spirit, but all His wondrous gifts as well, and especially the priceless gift of sanctifying grace which makes us partakers of God's intimate life and nature, capable of actions which are supernatural and divine, truly worthy of eternal life.

A Fine Example

If we ever have had to work long hours in an open field on a hot summer day, we know what a blessing it is to have a spring or a fountain of cool, clear water nearby. When a person is really thirsty, there is nothing lovelier to the eye or sweeter to the taste than good water. One feels as if new life were entering one's body with each mouthful—as if one were drinking in a fresh supply of life itself. Having been brought up in a hot, dry country, Jesus knew what it meant to be really thirsty; so did the Samaritan woman. He could scarcely have used a better example to explain to her that when God comes to live in a soul through grace, He becomes in its inmost depths an abiding fountain of everlasting life, a spring which never runs dry, but ever continues to flood the soul with the refreshing strength and presence of God.

Foretold by Jeremias

A fountain of living water in the depths of her soul! If the poor Samaritan woman had known the Scriptures, she might have remembered how God had called Himself a fountain of living water when He complained against His people, through the prophet Jeremias, saying: "They have forsaken *Me, the fountain of living water.*"[11] And if the

---

10 John 7, 37-39.
11 Jeremias 2, 13. See also Jeremias 17, 13; Ezechiel, chapter 47.

living water which Christ could give her could become a *fountain of living water* in her soul, then, surely it must be something of God, something able of itself to flood her soul with the living God.

"Like a Watered Garden"

If ever we had to walk or ride for hours over dunes of burning sand in the merciless heat of a vast desert, with not a sign of life as far as the eye can see, we would begin to understand what the absence of life means. And if we suddenly came upon a beautiful oasis covered with green trees and plants, we would begin to appreciate the worth and beauty of life. And what is it that changes a dry desert into a lovely, green oasis? Just a good supply of water. And, conversely, the lack of water changes a beautiful oasis into a dry desert. So it is with a human soul. Without sanctifying grace, a soul is like a barren, lifeless desert; but with grace, it is like an oasis, teeming with life; or, as the prophet Isaias says, "like a watered garden."[12]

Like Rain in Time of Drought

Perhaps we have never been in a real desert or seen an oasis. But most of us have had experience with a summer dry spell, when no rain fell for weeks and the sun scorched the grass to a crisp, while plants drooped and died and leaves fell from the trees before their time. Then came a soaking rain, like precious jewels from heaven, and the thirsty earth deeply drank its fill. Soon the drooping plants were fresh and full of life again and the grass soft and green. So it is with human souls in which God begins to live through grace. They awaken to a new life, like fields and gardens made lovely and green again by a good rain, after

12 Isaias 58, 11.

having been parched by sun and drought till lifeless and brown.

An Experience

As a student of Philosophy I was appointed sacristan of the seminary chapel. One day during Holy Week, the priest-sacristan gave me two lovely potted plants with large snow-white flowers on them—a species of hydrangea—to decorate the repository for Holy Thursday. On Good Friday I put the flowers in the sacristy, intending to use them to decorate the altar for Easter. That evening after night prayers, I went to the sacristy to make sure that everything was in order. Everything was, except the poor flowers. I had forgotten to water them! To my chagrin I now saw that they had not only wilted; but, being young and tender, with no woody substance to support them, they had slumped in their pots like so many soft rags. My heart sank as low as the flowers. What was I to tell the priest-sacristan? Well, I could not tell him anything then, for it was the time of strict silence. It would have to wait till morning. I poured a few glasses of water into the pots, though I did so more to ease my mind than to remedy matters, for in my judgment the plants were dead. I went to sleep with a heavy heart that night, rebuking myself for my thoughtlessness. The next morning, as soon as I was fully awake, the thought of the two dead plants came back to my mind like a wet cloud dampening my spirits. After the customary prayers and meditation, I went to the sacristy to prepare things for the services. As I entered, I suddenly stopped short, for in the place of the dead hydrangeas, there now stood two live ones, as fresh and lovely as ever. The water I had poured into their pots so unhopingly the night before had revived them completely. A closer examination disclosed that one showed no signs of its ordeal by thirst, while the other suffered just a bit of permanent damage along the edges of some of its leaves and petals. That Easter Sunday, as I looked at the flowers adorning the altar, I kept marveling how a little water had raised them up from the dust into which they had slumped as if dead.

Where Does Water End and Life Begin?

When we consider the importance of water to all forms of life, we understand how aptly Jesus compared the life of grace in the soul to an unfailing fountain of "living water." Though life and water are by no means the same thing, the relation between the two is so close that it is truly difficult to say where one ends and the other begins. Though the same is true of all forms of earthly life, let us, for the sake of simplicity, consider only plant life. We know that a plant cannot even begin to live without water, for only water can cause a seed to germinate. Once alive, a plant can stay vigorous and green only as long as it has plenty of water. As soon as it is cut off from its water supply, it begins to die. At first the leaves become soft and dull, and droop toward the earth, unable to support their own weight. Then, as they lose more moisture, they shrivel and dry up. And when finally the stem begins to wrinkle, we know that the plant is beyond help. From the first moment of its sprouting until the last green cell had died of thirst, the life of the plant had been so entirely dependent on water that we cannot draw a line between the two. Yet, the line does exist, for, though the two are inseparable, life is not water and water is not life.

The water, however, which Jesus promised to give our souls to drink is different. It not only sustains life, but, being *living* water, it *gives* life; in fact, it *is* life—something of the imperishable life of God Himself, able to make the soul "live forever" with "everlasting life."

[57]

The Holy Bible does not tell us what happened later to the Samaritan woman. But, knowing the goodness and power of Jesus, and the good dispositions in the heart of the woman, we may assume that she gave up her sinful way of life and did penance; and that Jesus, in turn, granted her request and gave her, through Baptism, His "living water" to drink, causing it to become in her "a fountain of water, springing up unto life everlasting." We may assume, too, that now, in heaven, her soul is fully satisfied and can never thirst again, for she is ever near the very Fountain of Life to whom she once gave a drink of water from Jacob's Well.

"God is light, and in Him is no darkness."
1 JOHN 1, 5.

"I am the light of the world. He who follows Me does not walk in the darkness, but will have the light of life."
JOHN 8, 12.

"...The Lord shall be unto thee for an everlasting light, and thy God for thy glory."
ISAIAS 60, 19.

"...What fellowship has light with darkness?"
2 CORINTHIANS 6, 14.

"Darkness compasseth me about...; and no man seeth me. Whom do I fear?"
ECCLESIASTICUS 23, 26.

"...their understanding clouded in darkness, estranged from the life of God."
EPHESIANS 4, 18.

Chapter VI

"FROM DARKNESS TO LIGHT"[1]

Light Opposed to Darkness

Light and darkness can never exist together. When the last rays of daylight fade away in the west, night falls and reigns in the world; but when the first light of dawn appears in the heavens, the darkness of the night begins to flee and soon daylight reigns again. And so it is with all opposites—heaven and hell, life and death, good and evil: they can never be reconciled. Neither can God and sin reign together in the same soul; for the one excludes the other. For God is the light of eternal life, while sin is the darkness of everlasting death.

Light Was the First Perfection in the World

In the very first lines of the Bible we read that when God made the world it was void and empty, and darkness reigned over it. So He made light, the first great perfection introduced into the world. "And God saw the light that it was good; and He divided the light from the darkness."[2] Light was the first thing in the world deserving to be called "good" by God. And as God went on gradually to put order into the world and to create the various forms of life, He saw that everything was "good." Only the chaos and the darkness of the void and empty earth before light was yet made, failed to merit this fine compliment of God.

---

1 ". . . that they may turn from darkness to light and from the dominion of Satan to God." —Acts 26, 18.

2 Genesis 1, 4; see also vv. 1-3.

Darkness is not evil in itself. Physically, darkness is really nothing. It is merely the absence of the marvelous good which we call light. Yet, because of its close association with many forms of evil, darkness is often considered an evil in itself. People dislike darkness because it so often means danger. A slight danger can become a very serious one in the dark. Evil men often take advantage of darkness to commit sins which they would never commit in the daytime. In the words of the Holy Bible, the typical sinner says to Himself: "Who seeth me? Darkness compasseth me about and the walls cover me, and no man seeth me. Whom do I fear?"[3] Darkness thus seems to befriend the wicked by hiding him from view and concealing his sins.

Darkness a Symbol of Evil

In their everyday conversation men have for ages regarded darkness as a symbol or image of evil. And God has meant it to be so, as we can easily gather from the Holy Bible, written under His own inspiration. There the word "darkness" is used so many times as another name, a synonym, for every kind of evil, physical as well as moral. Death, misfortune, ignorance, damnation—each merits the name of "darkness" or "night."[4]

---

3 Ecclesiasticus 23, 25-26. See also Job 24, 14-17; Proverbs 7, 6-23.

4 Death: ". . . a land of misery and darkness, where the shadow of death and no order, but everlasting horror dwelleth." —Job 10, 22; see also John 9, 4.

Misfortunes: "I expected good things, and evils are come upon me. I waited for light and darkness broke out." —Job 30, 26.

Ignorance: ". . . their understanding clouded in darkness, estranged trom the life of God through the ignorance that is in them." —Ephesians 4, 18.

Damnation: "Ungodly men . . . for whom the storm of darkness has been reserved forever." —Jude 4-13. See also Matthew 8, 12.

The Blackest Darkness Is Sin

But the blackest "darkness" of all, outside damnation itself, is the darkness of sin.[5] When Christ came into the world to destroy sin, He said, "I have come a light into the world, that whoever believes in Me may not remain in the darkness."[6] Sin is, moreover, the cause of every other kind of "darkness" in the world. Death, eternal damnation, suffering and misfortunes—all are consequences of sin.[7] St. Paul says that death is "the wages of sin."[8] Yet every evil in the world can be called "the wages of sin," for evil is the awful price mankind must continually pay for sin, original and actual. Sin is therefore *the* darkness which has brought every other shade and shadow of the darkness of evil into the world.

Light Is the Symbol of Good

As darkness is a symbol of sin and evil, light, on the contrary, is a symbol of all that is good, not only on earth but also in heaven. Moral goodness, wisdom and knowledge, the blessings of God, the glory of heaven, even God Himself, are often described in the Holy Bible with words meaning "light."[9]

---

5 "Let us therefore lay aside the works of darkness." —Romans 13, 12. See also, 1 John 2, 11.

6 John 12, 46.

7 Death: ". . . Through one man sin entered into the world and through sin death." —Romans 5, 12.

Damnation: "The Son of Man will send forth His angels, and they will gather . . . those who work iniquity, and cast them into the furnace of fire." —Matthew 13, 41, 42.

Suffering: "I will multiply thy sorrows . . . cursed is the earth in thy work; with labor and toil shalt thou eat thereof . . ." —Genesis 3, 16 and 17.

8 Romans 6, 23.

9 Virtue: "But the path of the just, as a shining light, goeth forwards and increaseth even to perfect day." —Proverbs 4, 18. See also 1 John 2, 10.

Wisdom: "Love the light of wisdom." —Wisdom 6, 23. "Who sendeth knowledge as the light." —Ecclesiasticus 24, 37.

Heaven: "Then the just will shine forth like the sun in the kingdom of their Father." —Matthew 13, 43. "For the glory of God lights it up, and the Lamb is the lamp thereof." —Apocalypse 21, 23.

Earthly Beauty Is Born of Light

Of all the impressions we receive through our senses, only light (and its counterpart, warmth) come from the heavens; the others—sound, feeling, taste and smell—come from the world. Light is the fairest thing in God's material creation, for it gives beauty to everything else in the world. All the beauty of color and form, of life and of motion, is born of light. In the dark, the loveliest rose appears no lovelier than the soil it grows in; the heavens no fairer than the mud at our feet. And if light were different, that which is lovely might be ugly instead. Imagine the faces of our loved ones if light were purple, or blue, or an eerie green instead of white! Diamonds, rubies, and every precious stone derive their sparkle, beauty, and most of their worth from light.[10]

Light Is the First-Born of God's Creative Hand

Life and light are the two greatest perfections in the world, the closest material imitations of the substance of God. Of these, life is the better, for the world was made for life. Yet life could not exist without light. So God made light before He made anything else in the world. It is, indeed, after matter itself, the first-born of His creative power. Light is, as it were, God's creative hand expressed in a material way, reaching out into the world to sustain life and fill the world with blessings. It is God's smile, so to speak, made visible to His creation, begetting the song of birds, the laughter of children, and love and friendship and the joy of living.

God Is "Light"

Light is so great a good in the world that God has seen fit to take its lovely name for Himself. "I am the light of

10 See Chapter VII, paragraph 1.

the world," He said.[11] Scientists estimate that we acquire nine-tenths of all our knowledge of the world through our eyes; that is, from light. It is with good reason then that Jesus calls Himself "the light of the world." For, what earthly light is to the world and to our eyes and minds, God is to our immortal souls. Without Him our souls would be immersed in the blackest spiritual darkness, without love, without hope, and without the beauty of the reflection of His Face.

God Is the Supernatural Light of the Soul

God created the marvel of light in order that life might exist and that our bodily eyes might be able to see and enjoy the works of His hands. But He knew that no created light would ever be bright enough and beautiful enough to satisfy our spiritual souls, made to His own image and likeness. So He deigned to become Himself the supernatural light of our souls, "the true light that enlightens every man who comes into the world,"[12] giving to all who receive Him the "power of becoming sons of God."[13] We call this light of God in our souls "sanctifying grace."

Sunlight not only illumines the world but is also the source of energy in living things, and consequently, of life itself. So, too, God not only enlightens the human mind by grace, but is also the source of new energy and a new life in the soul, "the life of God."[14] If earthly light, which is but a feeble imitation of the splendor of God, is such a marvelous thing, how wonderful must God Himself be! And if earthly light can make the world so beautiful, how

---

11 John 8, 12.
St. John says, "God is light, and in Him is no darkness." —1 John 1, 5.
12 John 1, 9.
13 John 1, 12.
14 ". . . You are not to walk as the Gentiles walk in the futility of their mind, having their understanding clouded in darkness, estranged from the life of God through the ignorance that is in them." —Ephesians 4, 17-18.

beautiful must be the human soul which God has deigned to fill with the glory of His own divine brightness!

Grace and Sin Compared to Light and Darkness

Let us imagine going into a beautiful garden, full of graceful trees and shrubs and the loveliest flowers of every color and description, all arranged in the finest order. How beautiful would this garden be in bright sunlight, with a clear blue sky overhead! But how different would this same garden be on an absolutely dark night! No visible color or beauty—nothing but blackness. Yet, the next morning the garden would be as lovely as ever, with not a shade of its visual beauty lost in the blackness of the night. So it is with the beauty of God's presence in the human soul. It is completely lost in the blackness and gloom of mortal sin. But when the sinner sincerely repents, it revives in all its glory. The Sacrament of Penance (or perfect contrition) restores the splendor and beauty of God's presence in the soul, just as sunlight restores the visible beauty and loveliness of a garden.

In the Sacred Scriptures

God often spoke in the Holy Scriptures about this gift of His divine light in the human soul. Long before the birth of Jesus, the prophet Isaias wrote, ". . . The Lord shall be unto thee for an everlasting light, and thy God for thy glory."[15] Holy Job spoke of this gift of divine light when he said, "Who will grant me that I might be according to the months past, according to the days in which God kept me, when His lamp shined over my head, and I walked by His light in darkness; as I was in the days of my youth, when God was secretly in my tabernacle; when the Almighty was with me?"[16] And Jesus Himself said, "I am the light of

---

15 Isaias 60, 19.
16 Job 29, 2-5.

[66]

the world. He who follows Me does not walk in darkness, but will have the light of life."[17] And those who believed in Him, He called the children of light.[18]

Many People Reject the Light of God's Grace

It is a sad thing that so few people really appreciate this wondrous gift of God's presence in their souls. Some people seem to prefer to live in the darkness of sin for weeks, months, and even years at a time. Some confess their sins but without true repentance, and soon return to their old vices. God has indeed called us "out of darkness into His marvelous light,"[19] but many prefer the darkness. As Jesus said, "The light has come into the world, yet men have loved the darkness rather than the light, for their works were evil. For everyone who does evil, hates the light."[20]

Saying those words, Jesus was speaking not only from divine knowledge but also from bitter experience. He well knew that a certain group of men hated Him intensely because He was "the light of the world" who had come to dispel the darkness of sin and evil. He foresaw, too, that their hatred and rancor would continue to grow until they would try at last to extinguish this heavenly "light;" they would crucify their own Redeemer. They did crucify Him, but this only made Him shine the more brightly as the light of the world. For the passion and death of Jesus gave Him the power to enter into the very hearts of men, and shine in them with the glory, beauty, and brightness of His everlasting light, the marvelous, incomprehensible "light" which transforms sinful men into sons of God, just as surely as sunlight changes night into day.

---

17 John 8, 12.
18 "While you have the light, believe in the light, that you may become sons of light." —John 12, 36. See also Luke 16, 8.
19 1 Peter 2, 9.
20 John 3, 19-20.

Chapter VII

A POOL OF WATER

The Soul Compared to Water

The Marvel of Light and Colors

White light, or daylight, is a combination of all the colors of the rainbow. As it strikes various earthly objects on its swift journey from the sun, it may be absorbed almost entirely and changed into heat, as it is by dull black objects; or it may be almost completely reflected, as by highly polished surfaces. Most objects, however, absorb certain colors from the combination and reflect the others. We see only the reflected ones. Thus leaves appear green because they reflect mostly the green portion of light, absorbing the other colors and using their energy to carry on the life processes of the tree or plant. A red flower, on the contrary, reflects red. Snow is white because it reflects all colors equally. Color is therefore a sensation produced in our eyes by the remnants of white light reflected or cast off by visible objects. The ability to thus modify daylight, absorbing or reflecting, defracting or diffusing it, belongs to the visible objects themselves. But the colors are not produced by the objects; they are only the unused portion of white light reflected by the objects.

Pure Water Is Colorless

Most things in the world have a definite color, but some are colorless, or almost so. The most common of such substances is water. Being practically colorless, pure water is very transparent. This means that light can pass through it easily, filling it with its sparkle and brightness.

Water Can Be Colored

Having no color of its own, water can easily be colored by other substances. For example, if we put a drop of blue ink into a glass of water, the ink spreads throughout the water and begins to reflect blue light, absorbing the other colors. This makes the glass of water appear blue. Similarly, red ink will make the water red, green ink will make it green, and a piece of dirt will make it dirty.

Our Comparison

We may compare our soul to a pool of water. For, in a spiritual sense, the soul has no color of its own, but acquires the color of whatever is in it, good or bad.

Mortal Sin

A pool of dirty water will stay dark and dirty even in the brightest sun. The impurities present in the water stop the sunlight and keep it from filling the water with the beauty of its light. In much the same way, original sin or personal mortal sin makes the soul dark and unclean, preventing God from filling it with the heavenly light of sanctifying grace. But if the soul has been baptized and is free from mortal sin, God lives within it, filling it with the brightness of His divine presence, just as sunlight fills a pool of clear water.

| CLEAN WATER IS LIKE A SOUL IN SANCTIFYING GRACE AND FREE FROM ALL SIN | CLOUDY WATER IS LIKE A SOUL IN VENIAL SIN | DIRTY WATER IS LIKE A SOUL IN MORTAL OR ORIGINAL SIN |

FIG. 4.

If we put a few drops of milk into a glass of clear water, the water will become cloudy, losing much of its transparency and clearness. And the more impurities we put into the water, the less clear it becomes. We can compare this to the effect of venial sin on a soul. Venial sin is like a temporary cloudiness in the soul, which does not destroy in it the supernatural light of God, but only makes it shine less clearly and less brightly.

Like a Reflection in a Pool

One of the big thrills of childhood is to be able to see the reflection of one's face in a pool of water. And every child who has had this experience knows that in order to have the best reflection, the water must be clear and calm. If it is dirty or disturbed, the image will not be as bright or may not even be visible. So it is with our souls. If the soul is clean and sinless, God sees His image in it very clearly and is well pleased with it. But if the soul is full of the uncleanness of sin, He can barely make out His divine likeness in it, or cannot see it at all. And the less clearly His image is reflected in a soul, the less He is pleased with it.

Purifying Water by Filtration

No matter how dirty water may be, it can be made crystal-clear by distilling or filtering it. The simplest way to filter water is to make it pass through a few feet of sand and gravel. As it slowly seeps through the sand, most of its impurities are left behind, wedged between the rough grains of sand. That is how drinking water is filtered before being pumped into homes in many cities. And spring water is so clear because it is well filtered by passing through a lot of soil on its way to the spring.

If we like to experiment, we can make a simple little water filter and see for ourselves how water is purified by passing through sand. All we need for this experiment is some clean, washed sand in a common flower pot. Before putting the sand into the pot, the opening in the bottom should be covered with a piece of sparse cloth to keep the sand from coming out. (Instead of the flower pot, one could use a tin can, a pail, or some other container provided with an opening at the bottom.) Now, if we pour dirty water over the sand in our filter, it will come out much cleaner through the opening at the bottom, because much of the dirt will have remained in the sand. Of course, in order to have a very good filter, the sand in it would have to be several feet deep.

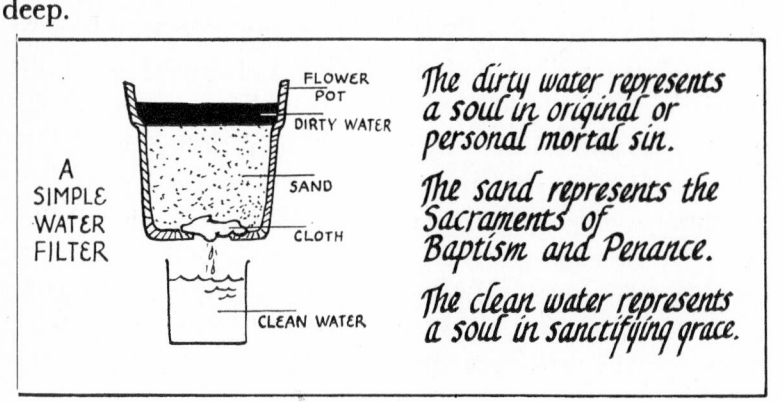

A SIMPLE WATER FILTER

FLOWER POT
DIRTY WATER
SAND
CLOTH
CLEAN WATER

The dirty water represents a soul in original or personal mortal sin.

The sand represents the Sacraments of Baptism and Penance.

The clean water represents a soul in sanctifying grace.

FIG. 5
Like the Sacraments

Our filter is like the Sacraments of Baptism and Penance. For, as a good filter removes the impurities from water and makes it crystal-clear, so the Sacraments of Penance and Baptism remove from the soul the impurities of sin, which were dimming or even blocking entirely the brightness of God's presence in the soul. Baptism removes the impurities of original sin and any actual sins committed before Baptism. Penance, on the other hand, can remove the impurities of any sins committed after Baptism. We might also add that the other Sacraments, especially Holy Communion, and also prayer and good deeds can remove the cloudiness of venial sin from the soul.

God Loves a Sinless Soul

We would never think of drinking dirty water. In fact, most people insist on clean water even to wash themselves in. Yet, these same people very often keep their immortal soul filled with the dirt of many sins, although they could keep it pure and clean by a frequent use of the Sacraments of Penance and Holy Communion, and by prayer and care in avoiding the occasions of sin.

It is always a pleasure to look at a crystal-clear brook, sparkling in the sunshine. So, too, it is a real pleasure for God to see a soul that is free from sin and filled with the heavenly sparkle of sanctifying grace. If water in a brook were human, it would probably complain that it has to flow over rough stones, sand and gravel. Yet it is these that help to make it clean and pure. So, too, many people complain that they have to deny themselves, suffer, and do penance for their sins. Yet these things are the spiritual stones, sand, and gravel that help to make and keep the soul pure and clean, worthy and fit to bear the reflection of God's face.

Our Noblest Task

A glass of water left uncovered in a dusty atmosphere soon becomes dirty. The same is true of our souls in this sinful world, full of scandals and temptations. No matter how much we try, our souls become tainted with various faults every day. We have to struggle all our lives to keep them clean. Yet we must never give up the struggle, for there is nothing more noble in the world than making and keeping our own souls a worthy dwelling place of God.

[73]

"Moses hid his face,
for he was afraid
to look at God."
EXODUS 3, 6

Chapter VIII

SANCTIFYING GRACE or GOD'S LIFE IN US

EXPLAINED WITH EXPERIMENTS

Introduction

We often hear, read, and speak about sanctifying grace. We know that it is a mysterious something which makes us children of God, holy and pleasing to Him, and heirs of heaven. We know, too, that it is God's greatest gift to us because our eternal happiness depends upon it entirely. Yet, in spite of our faith, and our knowledge and appreciation of this sublime gift of God, the mention of the term "sanctifying grace" usually leaves us cold and uninspired.

The reason for this is that the term "sanctifying grace" is a literal translation of the Latin "gratia sanctificans," which is a technical term used by theologians. Professional people usually have such special scientific names for various things in their line of work—names which other people often do not understand. Thus doctors have special names, usually Latin ones, for diseases; and naturalists have such names for plants and animals. Every branch of science in fact has its own list of scientific names. The same is true no less in the scientific study of religion, which we call theology. It, too, has its list of scientific names, and one of them is the term "sanctifying grace." Like a label in a scientific laboratory, it is accurate in meaning, but, unfortunately, lacking in the warmth, life, and color which a word so sublime in meaning might be expected to have.

Jesus Himself never used the expression "sanctifying grace." If He had, He would not have been understood by the simple people of His time. His words had to be simple and descriptive, capable of carrying the sublime meaning of His teachings into the hearts of even the most simple. And the word He preferred to use when explaining sanctifying grace was the word "life." That was His own best name for His own best gift to us. "I came that they may have *life*," He said, "and have it more abundantly."[1] He came into the world in order to bring the life of God into our souls after we had lost it through sin; and He called it by no other name except "life"—everlasting life.

It is so much easier to understand a thing if we can see it. A picture, it is said, can teach more than thousands of words. Jesus was well aware of this, and that is why He often used examples and stories in His divine teachings. Like a great artist, He masterfully painted pictures in people's minds and then used those pictures to teach them spiritual things. In this chapter we are going to imitate the Master's methods by trying to explain the hidden mystery of God's life in us with the help of visible earthly things in the form of simple little experiments.

I. Experiments with Water

We have already seen in other chapters of this book that sanctifying grace is God's gift of Himself to us. When we are in sanctifying grace, God is ours and we are His; He lives in us and we live in Him. On first thought this may sound like a contradiction, but a simple little experiment will show that it is not. If we drop a common sponge into

---

1 John 10, 10.

[76]

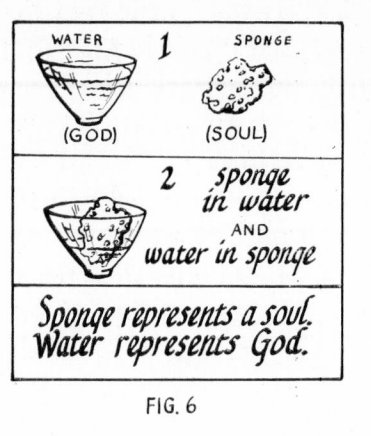

a dish of water, the sponge soaks up water, and soon we have a sponge in water and water in the sponge (Figure 6).

In the same way, if we are in sanctifying grace, God fills our souls as completely as the water in our experiment filled the sponge. He then truly lives in us and we in Him. For God is a spirit, and so is our soul; and two spirits can exist one within the other far more easily than any earthly substances.

Souls in Mortal Sin

While preaching about God to the pagan Athenians, St. Paul said, "He is not far from any one of us. For in Him we live and move and have our being."[2] God is at all times everywhere and in all things, and all things are in Him. Yet we often say that God leaves a soul when it commits a mortal sin. By this we do not mean that God goes out of the soul entirely, but rather that He is no longer on intimate terms with it, because it has purposely turned its back on Him. Though He continues to stay in such a soul, He cannot share His divine life with it, because of the obstacle of sin. His presence in the soul is not that of a father and friend, but that of a severe judge. The following experiment will explain this:

---

2 Acts 17, 27-28.

FIG. 7

Figure contents:

1 — GOD | SOUL | MORTAL SIN (TAR)

2 — WE PLUNGE THE SPONGE INTO TAR.

3 — WE PLACE THE TARRED SPONGE IN THE WATER.

4 — THE TARRED SPONGE DOES NOT SOAK UP THE WATER. THE SPONGE IS BLACK & STICKY AND DIRTIES EVERYTHING IT TOUCHES.

5 — *In the same way, mortal sin keeps God out of the soul, makes it ugly and dirties (by scandal) other people whom the sinner meets.*

Let us take a piece of dry sponge and dip it in tar.[3] Tar is ugly stuff—black, sticky, and smelly. We know that, because we sometimes get it on our clothes. The tar sticks to the sponge and makes the sponge itself look like tar. Now let us drop this tarred sponge into our dish of water. Does the sponge absorb any water? No, because the tar repels the water. So the sponge is in the water all right, but the water cannot wet the sponge (Figure 7).

The same is true of a soul in mortal sin. Mortal sin is like the black, greasy, ugly, ill-smelling tar; it repels God, just as tar repels water, and keeps Him from sharing His life with the soul. For God is all-holy, while mortal sin is the very opposite of holiness, and the two can never exist together in the same soul.

II. Experiments with Fire

"God Is a Consuming Fire."[4]

One day, long ago, about 1440 years before Christ was born, Moses was tending sheep on the slopes of Mount Horeb,[5] in Arabia. Suddenly he saw a strange sight, a living bush on fire on the mountainside. It was strange enough to

---

[3] Paint or any other dark, greasy substance will do. This and the preceding experiment need not actually be performed, since the facts will be evident to most.

[4] Hebrews 12, 29.

[5] Another name for Mount Sinai.

see a live, green bush burn so brightly; but stranger yet was the fact that the bush was not burnt or harmed in the least but remained fresh and green. Moses became very curious and said: "I will go and see this great sight, why the bush is not burnt."[6] But as he approached he heard a voice from the burning bush: "I am the God of thy father, the God of Abraham, the God of Isaac, and the God of Jacob."[7] When Moses realized that God was appearing to him in the form of a fire in the bush, he became frightened and hid his face, not daring to look at the flame. But God spoke kindly to him and sent him into Egypt to lead the Hebrew people into the Promised Land.

We see many strange and wonderful things today—things which Moses never even dreamed of. We are so used to automobiles, trains, airplanes, electricity, and so on, that we pay little attention to them. But if we should see a green bush burning brightly without getting burnt, we would be as wide-eyed with wonder as Moses was. For we would know that it was something miraculous, since an earthly fire can exist only when it is consuming something. Yet, there is something even more marvelous than the burning bush happening within us every day.

For the same great God who appeared to Moses in the burning bush actually lives in every human soul which is in the state of sanctifying grace. Just as the fire made the bush bright and warm, like a real fire, so God makes the soul beautiful and good, as He is Himself, in so far as this is possible for a creature. A soul in sanctifying grace does not cease to be a soul, just as the bush did not cease to be a bush. But since it now has God living in itself, it also looks like Him and is truly His child.

---

6 Exodus 3, 3.
7 Exodus 3, 6.

In order to explain how these wonderful things happen in the soul, we are now going to perform some little experiments with fire taken directly from the sun, comparing God's presence in our soul through grace to fire in a piece of charcoal.

A "Real Image" of the Sun

The first experiment in this group will be an introductory one. For it, we need a magnifying glass, a sheet of paper, a bright sun in the sky and, of course, a room on the sunny side of the building. If we hold the sheet of paper parallel to a window in the room, and our magnifying glass between the window and the sheet of paper, parallel to both and at the proper distance from the paper (usually a few inches), we can see a perfect upside-down image of the window on the sheet of paper. And if someone stands at the window, his image will also appear (upside down) on the sheet of paper. (In the study of optics, we call this image a *real image*.) Now if we change our position so that we are directly in line with the sun as it appears in the window,

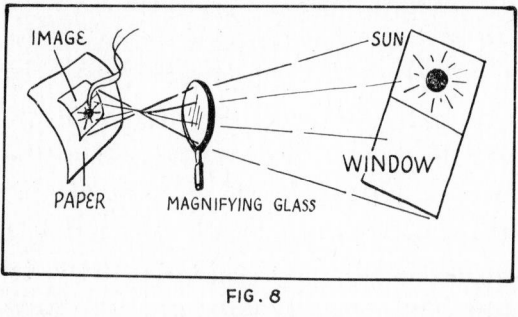

FIG. 8

the image of the sun will also appear on the sheet of paper. (See Figure 8.) And if we move our magnifying glass slowly toward the paper and away from it, we notice that when the image of the sun is most perfect on the sheet of paper, the paper begins to burn in that spot. This means that when the image of the sun is most perfect on the paper, the paper itself becomes at that point like a tiny sun, bright and hot.[8]

In much the same way, sanctifying grace imprints the true image of God in our souls, making our souls like God by giving us a share in His divine life and nature.

Experiments with Charcoal:
Preliminary Explanations

Our next experiments will be experiments with actual fire derived from the sun. They are not going to be as wonderful as the burning bush that Moses saw, but will be quite interesting. For these experiments we need a few pieces of dry charcoal, some incense, a magnifying glass, a mirror, a nice bright sun in the sky, and a room on the sunny side of the building. We place the pieces of charcoal on small dishes or ashtrays on a desk or table where everybody can see them. Then we place a flat-surface mirror on the window sill or some other convenient place so that it reflects the sunlight to our table. The purpose of the mirror is to direct the sunlight to our table. Now, if we hold the magnifying glass in the path of sunlight reflected by the mirror, so that the sunlight passes through the magnifying glass and is focused[9] on a piece of charcoal, the charcoal begins to burn almost immediately and soon becomes a glowing, red-hot coal. If it burns too slowly, we can fan it or blow on it gently after it has started to burn.

The sun is like an immense ball of atomic fire, radiating heat and light in every direction. The following illustration

---

8 To avoid eye discomfort, use sunglasses for this experiment, for the "true image" of the sun on the paper can hurt the eyes, though not as much as the sun itself.

9 See Author's Introduction, No. 11.

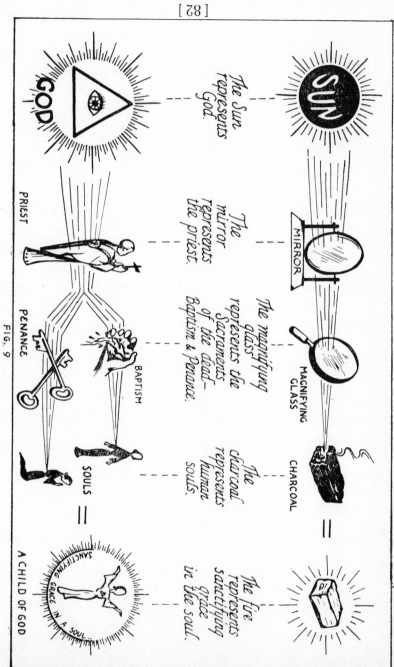

FIG. 9

(Figure 9) shows how, when some of the rays coming from this huge ball of fire were reflected by the mirror and focused on the charcoal by the magnifying glass, the charcoal began to burn and itself became a piece of fire. We can say, therefore, that fire from the sun entered the piece of charcoal and changed it into a tiny sun, hot and bright.

Figure 9 also shows how sanctifying grace is something of God which comes into the soul, chiefly through the sacraments administered by God's priests, and transforms it into a child of God, thus making it holy and pleasing to Him.

The Preceding Illustration (Figure 9) Explained in Detail

FIG. 10

We compared God to the sun; as practically all energy, light, and warmth come from the sun and make life possible in the world, so sanctifying grace comes from God and gives a new life to the soul, a true share in God's life (Figure 10).

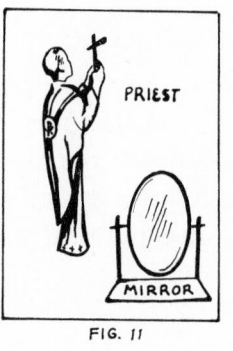

FIG. 11

We compared the priest to a mirror, because as a mirror can reflect sunlight to any place we wish, so the priest can administer the sacraments to individual souls. God normally gives the gift of His life to souls through the sacraments, but there must be a priest to administer the sacraments. The priest thus stands between God and the sacraments just as the mirror stands between the sun and the magnifying glass (Figure 11).

[83]

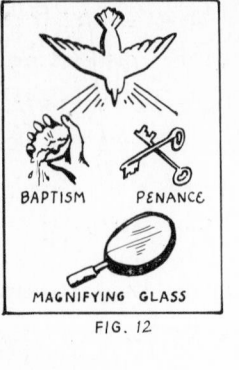

BAPTISM   PENANCE

MAGNIFYING GLASS

FIG. 12

We compared the sacraments to a magnifying glass; as the magnifying glass concentrates the sunlight in one spot, causing it to ignite each piece of charcoal, so the sacraments, when worthily received, bring the life of God to each soul, as if concentrating the presence of the infinite God within the narrow limits of the soul (Figure 12). And as the magnifying glass forms an image of the sun on the charcoal, making the charcoal like a little sun, so the sacraments imprint the image of God on the soul, making it like God.

SOUL

CHARCOAL

FIG. 13

We compared the soul to a piece of charcoal, because as charcoal can receive heat and light from the sun and be changed into fire, so the soul can receive God's life and be changed into a child of God (Figure 13).

FIG. 14

We compared sanctifying grace to fire; just as fire from the sun enters the charcoal and changes it into a tiny sun, hot and bright, so sanctifying grace is something of God entering the soul and changing it into a true child of God (Figure 14). And as the burning charcoal is both charcoal and fire at the same time, so the soul in sanctifying grace has both a natural and a supernatural life at the same time.

With the exception of Christ and His Mother, all people begin their earthly existence in the sorry state of original sin.[10] They are therefore born without sanctifying grace and are mere creatures, not children of God.

This part of our experiment explains the condition of souls in original sin. We begin the experiment with four pieces of charcoal. They are all cold, hard, black, and dirty (Figure 15).

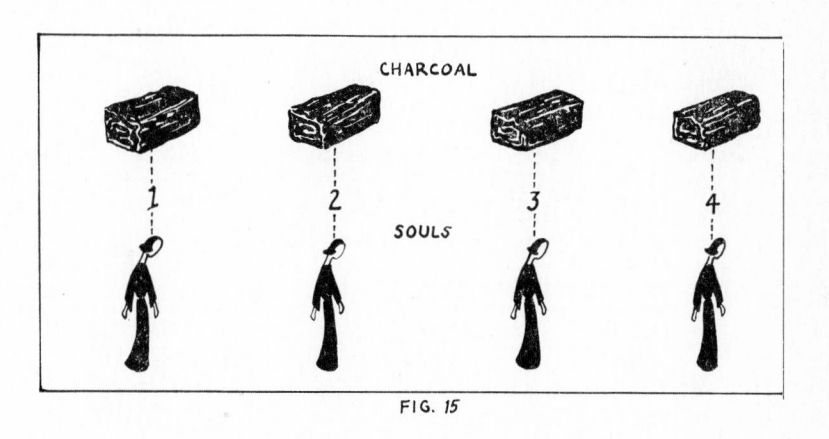

CHARCOAL

SOULS

FIG. 15

The four pieces of charcoal represent four persons who have never been baptized. They are in original sin and are perhaps burdened with many sins of their own (if they have already arrived at the use of reason). These sins make their souls ugly, dirty, cold and hard before God—like the pieces of charcoal. Spiritually speaking, they are completely dead, turned away from God, and lost.

---

10 Christ was free from original sin because He was God. His Mother was free from it because God gave her this special favor; we call it the Immaculate Conception. Theologians commonly teach that St. John the Baptist, though conceived in original sin, was cleansed from it at the time of the Visitation.

This part of our experiment explains how **Baptism** removes original sin and all personal sins which the soul may have committed.

Using our magnifying glass as explained above, we now light three of the four pieces of charcoal. They soon become red-hot, and bright, like tiny suns. They are still coals, but now they are live coals. We did not light the fourth piece; so it is still hard, cold, black, and dirty as ever (**Figure 16**):

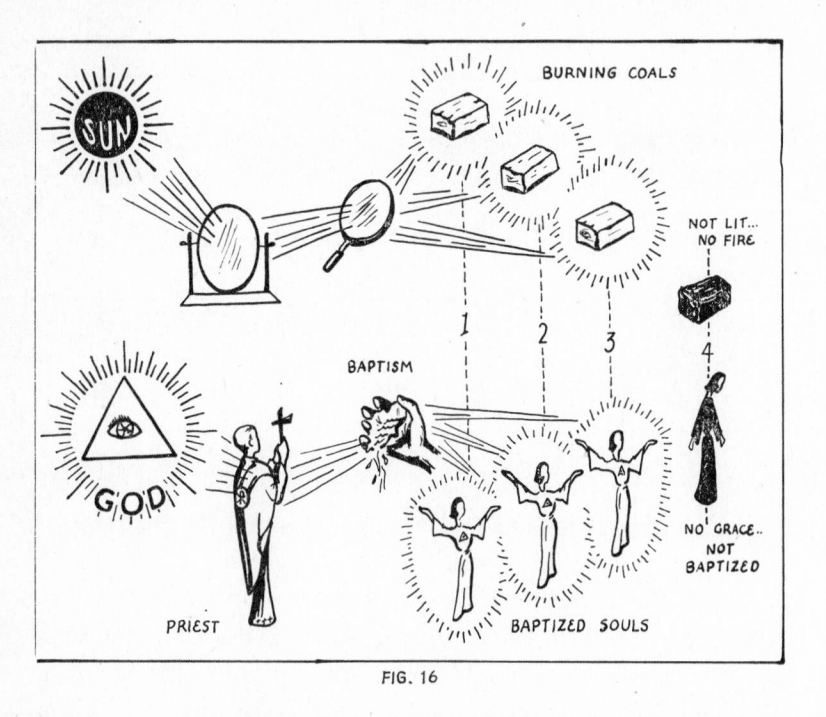

FIG. 16

The three burning pieces in Figure 16 represent three persons who have now been baptized and are in sanctifying grace. They are like God and are His children and dear friends. They are now clean, pure, beautiful, and pleasing to God. They are alive with God's life, and are heavenly

[86]

princes and princesses, worthy of heaven itself. Needless to say, God loves them dearly.

The fourth piece of charcoal represents the soul of one person out of the four, who was not baptized with the others. This soul is still dead in sin.

Part 3: Prayers and Good Deeds

The prayers and good deeds of souls in sanctifying grace merit a great reward in heaven. Those of souls in original sin do not merit any heavenly reward (although God may reward them with earthly blessings in this life). This part of our experiment explains this.

We now drop a bit of incense on each of the four pieces of charcoal. The incense burns readily on the three burning coals, emitting a white smoke which rises into the air and fills the room with a delightful fragrance. The incense does not burn on the fourth piece, which has no fire. Consequently, it does not give off any pleasant odor but is only wasted (Figure 17):

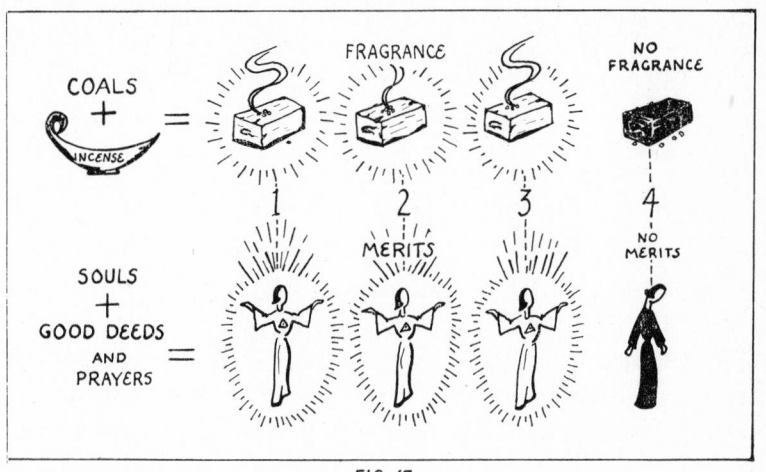

FIG. 17

In the Holy Bible, the rising smoke of incense represents prayers rising to God. Thus we read in one of the Psalms: "Let my prayer be directed as incense in Thy sight."[11] In our experiment the incense represents both the prayers and good deeds of the faithful.

The good deeds and prayers of souls in sanctifying grace are very pleasing to God. They rise up to Him like the fragrant smoke of incense and He will reward them greatly in heaven.

The good deeds and prayers of souls in original sin do not rise up to God like fragrant incense. Being spiritually dead through sin, such souls are unable to merit any heavenly reward.

Part 4: Personal Mortal Sin

Mortal sin causes the life of God to disappear from the soul. And when that happens, all the good deeds and prayers of the past are lost, until the sinner sincerely repents in the Sacrament of Penance (or through an act of perfect contrition). For the same reason, the soul cannot gain any new merits for heaven while in mortal sin. This part of our experiment will explain this.

Let us pour a few drops of water on two of the burning coals. What happens? The fire goes out and the two pieces of charcoal become cold, black, and dirty again. In fact, they are in a worse condition than before they were lit, because now they are all wet and messy, covered with ugly, gray ashes (Figure 18).

---

11 Psalm 140, 2.

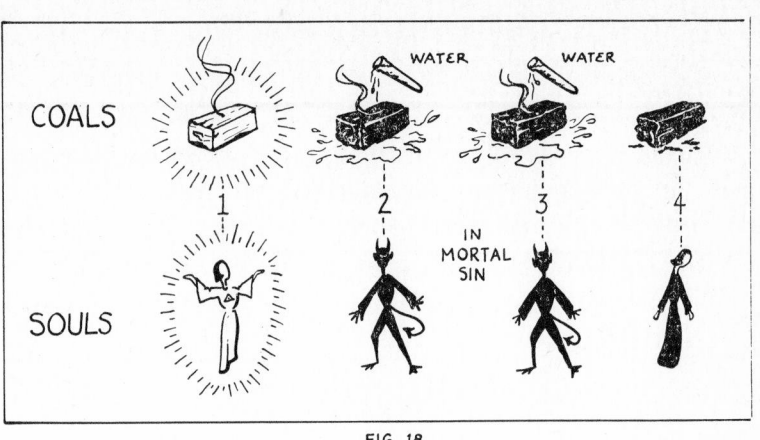

FIG. 18

Water on burning charcoal is like mortal sin in a soul.[12] What water does to a fire, mortal sin does to the life of God in the soul. Mortal sin makes the soul even more ugly and dirty than it was before Baptism with just original sin; because mortal sins committed after Baptism are worse than original sin and do more harm to the soul.

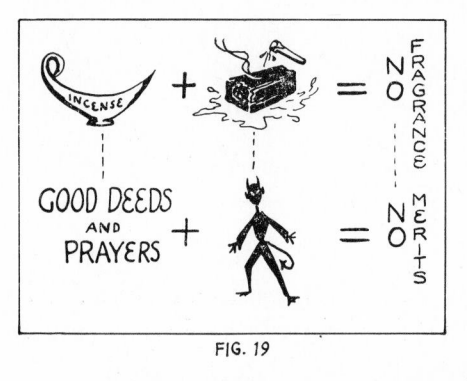

FIG. 19

If we put incense on the pieces of wet charcoal, the incense becomes wet and dirty, but will not burn or give off a pleasant odor (Figure 19).

This means that the good deeds and prayers of souls in mortal sin cannot please God or merit any heavenly reward.

12 This part of our experiment is not to be confused with the sponge and water experiments. There we compared God to water, and sin to tar. Here we compare grace to fire, and sin to water. There is **no connection** between the two experiments. The lesson we wish to convey in either case is that grace and mortal sin are two opposites which cannot co-exist in the soul.

Part 5: Penance (Confession)

By receiving the Sacrament of Penance worthily, we regain sanctifying grace as well as our lost merits. That is, we regain the supernatural worth of the prayers we had said and the good deeds we had done in the past while in the state of sanctifying grace, but which we had later lost through mortal sin. This part of our experiment will explain how we regain sanctifying grace through the Sacrament of Penance.

(1) A Bad Confession

Let us take our magnifying glass and try to light the pieces of wet charcoal. Yes, it is foolish even to try. They may steam a bit but will never burn (Figure 20).

FIG. 20

Wet charcoal is like a person who has mortal sins on his conscience but is not truly sorry for them. Even if he confesses them, they are not forgiven and he does not regain the gift of God's life or his lost merits of the past.

(2) A Good Confession

So we dry one of the pieces of charcoal[13] and try to light

---

[13] Since it takes some time to dry a piece of charcoal, one previously dried should be used.

it again. It burns as before; and incense placed upon it burns too, rising in fragrant smoke (Figure 21).

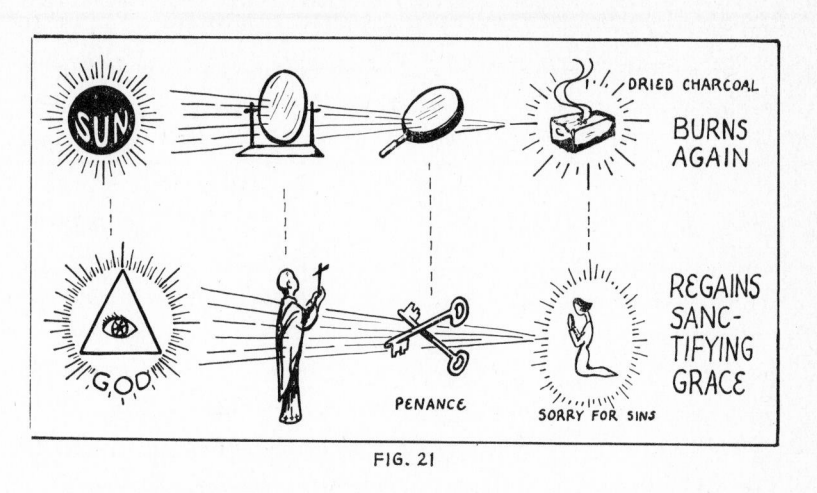

FIG. 21

Drying the charcoal is like being sorry for our sins. And lighting the dried charcoal is like being absolved from our sins when we are really sorry for them. As dried charcoal can be made to burn again, so, if we are truly sorry, our sins can be forgiven and we can regain the life of God in the Sacrament of Penance.

Confessing When Not in Mortal Sin

If we focus the sunlight on a piece of charcoal which is already burning, it will burn even better, and its fire will not go out as easily, because of the extra heat. In the same way, it we make our Confession when we have no mortal sin on our souls, we receive more sanctifying grace and extra help to avoid sin in the future.

Part 6: Holy Communion

In our next experiment we shall see how Holy Communion gives us more sanctifying grace—that is, a bigger share in God's life—and keeps us from losing it through mortal sin. (Be sure to read carefully No. 12 of the Author's Introduction before attempting this experiment.)

After lighting the charcoal, we may notice that it burns rather slowly and not too brightly. So we prepare some oxygen to make it burn better. We heat potassium chlorate and manganese dioxide in a pyrex test tube over a small flame. For this purpose we can use a candle, a cigarette lighter, a gas burner, or an alcohol lamp. A thimbleful of the potassium chlorate and about one-eighth as much of the manganese dioxide, mixed well together, will do. When heated sufficiently, these chemicals give off oxygen which flows through a small rubber tube to the burning charcoal. (See Figure 22.) The oxygen makes the burning charcoal flare up immediately and burn intensely. It becomes very bright and hot, actually white-hot, and really looks like a tiny sun now.[14]

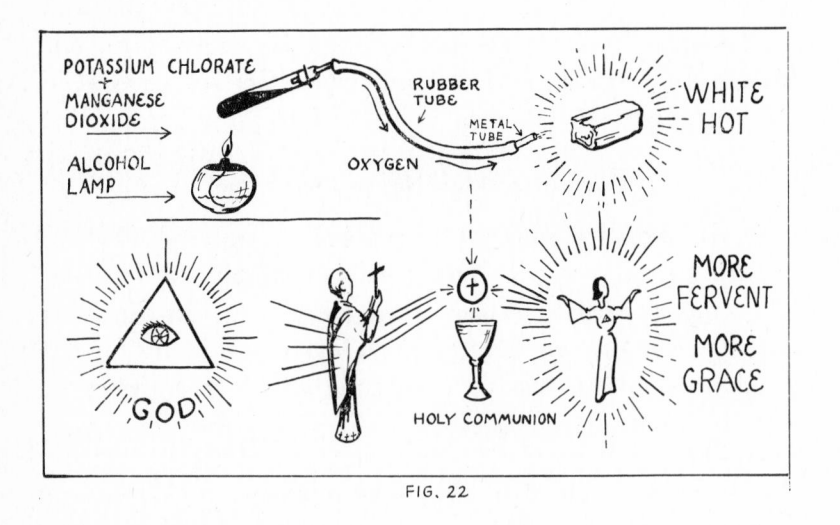

FIG. 22

---

[14] Blowing on the charcoal produces a similar (though inferior) effect by forcing oxygen present in the air against the fire.

An ordinary soul in sanctifying grace can be compared to a burning coal before oxygen has been added. Though this soul has God's life within itself, it may not be very fervent and may even be on the verge of losing its treasure of grace through sin: we may compare it to a fire that is slowly going out. But when this soul devoutly receives Holy Communion, it becomes like the charcoal after oxygen has been added. For just as a fire becomes brighter and much more like the sun when we add oxygen, so our souls become much more like God when we receive Holy Communion fervently and worthily. For Holy Communion, received with the right dispositions, makes the life of God "flare up" in the soul, so to speak, by giving us more sanctifying grace and uniting us more closely with God. And this in turn disposes the soul to be more fervent in loving God and more zealous in serving Him.

Receiving Holy Communion in Mortal Sin

If we let some oxygen flow onto a piece of charcoal that has no fire, the oxygen is only wasted and the charcoal remains unchanged—cold, black, and dirty (Figure 23).

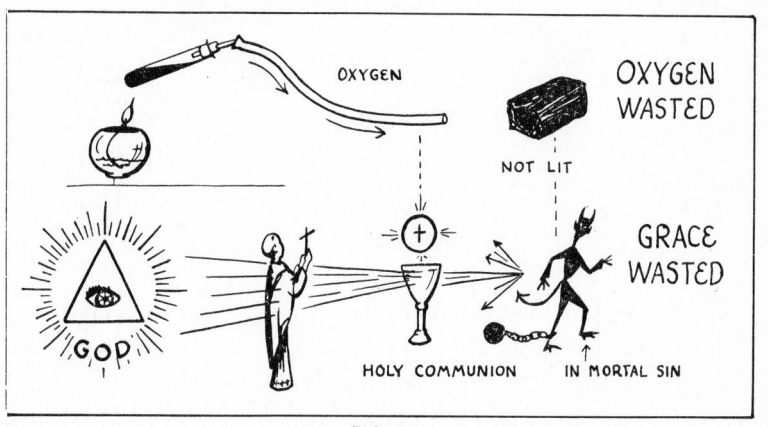

FIG. 23

In the same way, if a soul in mortal sin receives **Holy Communion**, this wonderful sacrament does not do the soul any good but is only wasted. Moreover, the soul commits a very serious sin of sacrilege, which makes it more ugly than ever.

Other Sacraments of the Living

In the oxygen experiment we spoke of the increase of sanctifying grace through Holy Communion. However, since Confirmation, Holy Orders, Matrimony, and Extreme Unction, besides producing their own special effects, also increase sanctifying grace in the soul, the experiment can be used to apply to them too.

Part 7: Conclusion

(I) A Final Comparison

Now that we have finished our experiments, let us take one more look at our four pieces of charcoal and the four souls they represent, carefully noting the difference between them.

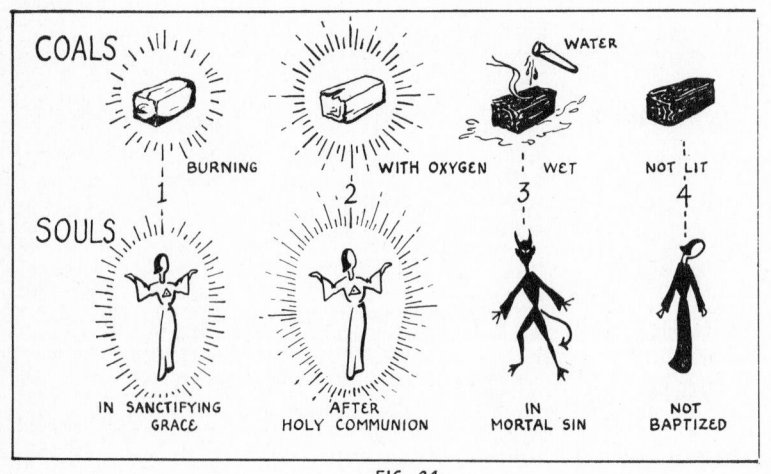

FIG. 24

[94]

The souls represented in Figure 24 are souls of living persons who must die some day. Let us suppose that they die in the condition in which they are shown above. What will happen to them? The next part will tell us.

(2) Heaven or Hell?

We have seen in our experiments how the sun changed dirty, black coals into live ones, hot and bright. On special occasions, God's priests take such coals to the altar and burn incense upon them to honor God.

A priest cannot use at the altar charcoal that has no fire within it—much less if it is wet—so he does not take it to the altar but puts it aside, either into the charcoal box or the waste basket, depending on its condition (Figure 25).

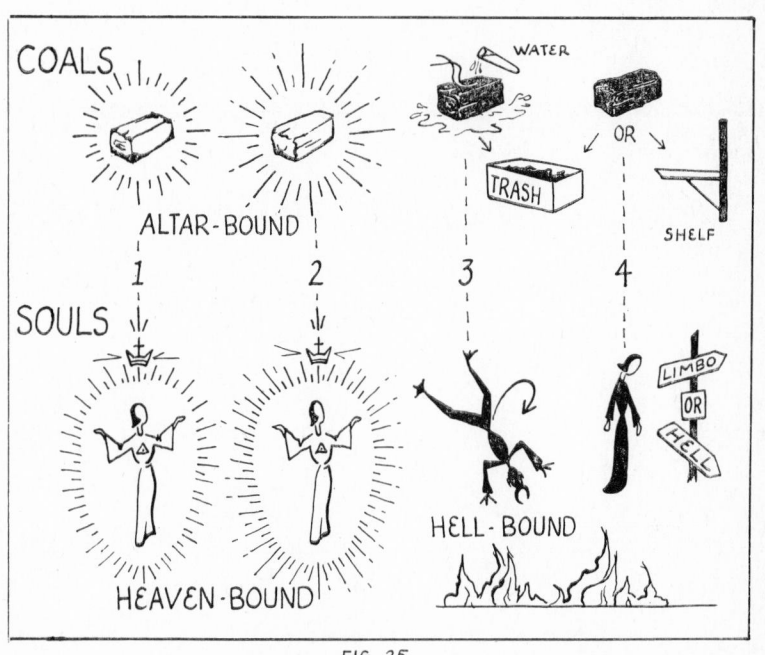

FIG. 25

We have seen from the experiments and explanations how God changes human souls into His own children through sanctifying grace. He loves such souls dearly because they are alive with His own life and are very beautiful in His sight, since they are like Him. When they die He takes them to His beautiful heaven, where they will love Him and please Him forever with the fragrance of the good they did while living on earth in the state of sanctifying grace.

Souls in mortal sin, on the contrary, are as worthless in the sight of God as a piece of wet charcoal is to a priest at the altar. So God throws them away to smolder forever on the "rubbish pile" of hell.

Chapter IX

A BOUQUET OF FLOWERS

Grace Is a Fragrance: Sin Is a Bad Odor

Johnny had received an aquarium with tropical fish in it as a Christmas gift. He kept them proudly in his room and took good care of them. They were a very pretty sight, with their bright colors and varied sizes and shapes. Johnny spent many happy moments at the aquarium, feeding the fish and watching them frisk and play in the clear water. Finally, summer came and Johnny's parents decided to take a trip. Johnny was going to leave the fish with a neighbor while he was gone, but in the excitement he forgot to do so.

When Johnny returned from his vacation trip, he was heartbroken, for all his little fish were dead. Once so lovely, they were a miserable sight now. And what an odor in his room! He had to hold his nose upon entering. But his mother knew just what to do. She took the aquarium out of the room and opened the windows wide. And in a short time most of the bad odor was gone. Then she went into the garden and cut a large bouquet of fragrant flowers and placed them in a vase in the very spot where the aquarium had been.

That evening after supper Johnny's uncle dropped in for a visit, and seeing the boy's grief, he took the aquarium away, promising to bring it back the very next day, all cleaned and sterilized, and stocked with live fish from his own collection. Needless to say, the lad soon forgot his loss and his grief.

When Johnny went to his room to sleep that night, there was no trace of the bad odor, but instead the sweet fragrance of the flowers. So Johnny was able to expand his lungs and breathe in deeply of the fresh and fragrant air, whereas only a short time ago the room had reeked of a most unpleasant odor. Then he knelt down, thanked God for a safe journey, jumped into bed, and was soon fast asleep.

It is a good thing to be able to change the air in our room from foul to fresh in such a short time. But, to be able to change our soul from ugly to beautiful in perhaps an even shorter time, is truly wonderful. For, the room in our story is our own soul, and the bad odor in the room is mortal sin. The fresh, clean and fragrant air on the other hand is sanctifying grace.

We know that whatever dies in this world, soon begins to decompose, giving off unpleasant odors in the process, like the poor little fish in our story. Now, a soul in mortal sin is spiritually dead, having lost its supernatural life. To be sure, there is nothing in the soul to give forth an odor or to decay, for the soul is a spiritual substance with a natural life which is immortal. Nevertheless, mortal sin fills the soul with so much spiritual uncleanness that it becomes, spiritually speaking, as disgusting to God as a decaying animal is to our eyes and nostrils. The death and decay of a human body is, in fact, the penalty for sin. And Jesus Himself compared sin to the contents of a sepulchre when He said: "Woe to you, Scribes and Pharisees, hypocrites! because you are like whited sepulchres, which outwardly appear to men beautiful, but within are full of dead men's bones and of all uncleanness."[1] Figuratively and humanly speaking, God would have to hold His nose if He wanted to remain in a soul in mortal sin.

---

1 Matthew 23, 27.

Happily for us, if we are truly sorry for our sins and make a good confession, mortal sin disappears from our souls, just as a bad odor disappears from a room when we open the windows. Moreover, God comes to live in our souls again, filling them with His divine presence, just as the fragrance of flowers fills a room. If we place a bouquet of roses in a room, the room will smell like roses. Lilies will make it smell like lilies, and so on. So it is with our souls. When God fills them with the sweet fragrance of His presence, they become like God Himself. We call this fragrance of God in our souls "sanctifying grace," or God's life in us.

What great care should we take to live continually in sanctifying grace, that our soul may never reek of the God-repelling odor of mortal sin, but rather that it may always be pleasing to Him, filled with the delicate fragrance of His divine presence!

Chapter X

A SKUNK IN THE CLASSROOM

A Story Illustrating the Difference between Mortal and Venial Sin

Contrary to what we may think, a little skunk, with its glossy black coat, white stripes and bushy tail, is really a cute little animal. And it is quite friendly, too. But it has one very bad habit. Whenever it becomes alarmed or frightened, it makes itself unbearable by releasing a liquid with a very offensive smell. God gave it this power for its self-defense, to protect it against its enemies. But, unfortunately, the poor skunk sometimes harms its friends in this way, thinking they are enemies. As a result, it has very few friends and a very bad name.

We rarely find skunks in large cities. People just do not trust them and will not have them around. There are many skunks in the open country, however. Sometimes they make their dens under farm buildings.

One year a family of skunks made its home near a small, one-room country school. As soon as the baby skunks were big enough, Mamma Skunk began to take them out to teach them how to hunt for food. Usually this was at night, but sometimes even in broad daylight. No doubt she also taught them how to defend themselves in traditional skunk fashion.

One day the whole family of skunks took an afternoon stroll. Their line of march took them near the school. The children could not see them but knew they were there because of the odor coming in through an open window. The odor was not very strong—just some of the scent adhering to the skunks' coat from a previous engagement; so the children only smiled and held their noses, and the girls giggled as usual.

As the children were used to skunks, they soon forgot all about them—that is, all except two of the bigger boys. These boys were always looking for mischief and the skunks gave them an idea. That evening the boys went to the school grounds and set a box trap, the kind that would catch a skunk without hurting him. Then they sat down and waited. Before long, one of the little ones came out of the den. The boys could see him in the bright moonlight. He raised his little nose and sniffed the air. He had smelled the piece of raw meat in the trap. He came closer and closer, sniffing all the while, until he had walked right into the trap. The boys then slowly released a string they were holding and the trap closed so quietly that the skunk didn't quite realize his plight.

The boys then carried the box carefully to the school building and entered through a window. Then they opened the door of a closet a little, slipped the trap partly into the closet, and opened the door of the trap. By this time the little skunk had finished the meat in the trap and was sniffing about for more. The boys threw a piece into the closet and in a few seconds the skunk's keen little nose had led him through the open door of the trap to the far end of the closet. The boys then gently withdrew the trap, closed the closet door, and went home. The little skunk did not even know that he had been "kidnapped." He finished the piece of meat, licked his chops, and went to sleep in a corner of the closet.

The next day school began as usual. No one noticed the little striped visitor sleeping comfortably in the closet corner behind a waste basket. The two boys eyed the closet nervously, expecting a climax any minute. Finally the teacher went to the closet to get her handkerchief from her coat pocket. The two boys almost froze with fear. This would be *it,* and their doom besides. But still nothing happened. The teacher walked away, leaving the closet door partly open.

It was a warm day in late spring and the outside door of the school was wide open. The skunk, disturbed by the classroom noises, awoke, stood up and stretched. And then, seeing the open door, he decided to go home to his mother. He crept out of the closet and started playfully across the classroom floor toward the open door leading to the outside and to freedom. He might have escaped unnoticed, except for a girl in the front seat. Seeing the skunk in front of her desk, she screamed and jumped up onto a desk. All the other girls and the teacher did likewise, scarcely knowing why. This was the usual procedure in those days whenever a mouse ventured into the classroom. The poor little skunk was not used to such screaming and sudden action. He froze in his tracks, frightened out of his wits, thinking that the girls were all going to pounce down upon him from their desks. Poor little fellow! He could not really help it, but what an odor filled the room as he finally darted out through the open door!

It was only a matter of seconds before all the children darted out even faster through the same door; not chasing him but trying to escape from the sickening fumes.

It took a lot of airing, scrubbing and fumigating before all the odor was gone from the classroom. In the meantime, classes were held outside, in the shade of a large elm tree. Frankly, everybody enjoyed it. No one ever found out how the skunk had entered the classroom. Since the outside door was open, they supposed that he had just walked in when no one was looking. However, the teacher did notice that two boys in her class were unusually quiet for almost two weeks, and she wondered why.

The Meaning of Our Story

The classroom in our little story represents our own soul. The offensive odor of the skunk represents sin, and the children in the classroom represent sanctifying grace. The story illustrates the simple doctrine of mortal and venial sin as found in the catechism. First of all, it illustrates the big difference in the effects of venial and mortal sin on the soul.

Venial Sin

When a little of the odor drifted into the classroom through the open window, the children merely held their noses. The smell was unpleasant but bearable, and was soon gone and forgotten, carried away by a current of fresh air. The same is true of venial sin in the soul. It harms the soul but does not destroy grace. God dislikes it, but bears with it and continues to dwell in the soul. The bad effects of venial sin are temporary and can be undone by the "fresh air" of good deeds, prayer, and the practice of virtue.

Mortal Sin

However, when the classroom was filled with the full-strength skunk odor, it was an entirely different matter. Everybody ran out pellmell, and stayed out, for the odor remained stubbornly in the classroom. So it is with mortal sin in the soul. Humanly speaking, it is so offensive and displeasing to God that He has to leave the soul. And when God is gone, the soul, robbed of divine life, becomes as dismal and dead as a classroom without children. This effect is quite permanent too, and can be undone only through the "scrubbing" of sincere contrition and the Sacrament of Penance. In other words, God stays out of the soul, till it decides to clean up the mess.

The Three Conditions for Mortal Sin:
Seriousness of the Wrong Done

Secondly, our story illustrates the three conditions necessary to make a sin mortal. The first of these conditions is the seriousness of the wrong done. This is the most important of the three because a sin can never be serious unless the wrong done is serious, at least in the mind of the sinner.[1] In our story this condition is illustrated by the seriousness of the contamination of the classroom. A slight contamination represents venial sin, which does comparatively little harm to the soul. A serious contamination made the classroom unfit for occupation, just as mortal sin makes the soul unfit to be a dwelling place or temple of God.

Knowledge and Consent

The second and third conditions of mortal sin are full knowledge and full consent. This means that the sinner must know that a certain sin is serious and must nevertheless commit it freely and deliberately. In our story these two conditions are illustrated by the two mischievous boys. They were well aware of the possible serious consequences of their action, yet they did it freely and deliberately, with forethought and reflection, and were consequently fully responsible for their action.

If one or more of the above three conditions is not fulfilled in a given sin, the sin is not mortal. This means that even though the matter involved is serious, if either full knowledge or full consent is lacking, the sin is venial.

(Another explanation of the difference between mortal and venial sin will be found in the next chapter, where sin is compared to poison.)

---

1 A certain action, thought, word, or omission may be, objectively speaking, a venial sin or no sin at all. Yet, if a person considers it serious and does it deliberately, he is guilty of serious sin because he deliberately consents to what in his mind is a big sin.

Chapter XI

SIN IS SPIRITUAL POISON

Mortal Sin

All deliberate sin, whether mortal or venial, is a great evil. Of the two, mortal sin is by far the greater. Mortal sin is so great a wrong that it forces God out of the soul, depriving the soul of His wondrous grace and friendship. It is thus the seed or beginning of damnation in the soul, just as grace is the seed of heavenly glory. And for this reason mortal sin is truly the greatest misfortune that can ever befall the human soul in this world.

Venial Sin

Compared to mortal sin, venial sin is clearly a far lesser evil, for it can never deprive the soul of supernatural life, regardless of the kind or number of venial sins committed. This does not mean that venial sin should be taken lightly, especially deliberate venial sin; because, after mortal sin, it is surely the next greatest evil in the world. It displeases God who loves us and died for us, and its harmful effects on the soul are often far-reaching. For, besides decreasing the soul's fervor in God's service, and deserving temporal punishment, venial sin weakens the soul's resistance to evil and so paves the way for mortal sin, just as sickness weakens the body and prepares the way for death.

There is, indeed, as close a similarity between sickness and venial sin as there is between death and mortal sin. Perhaps in God's eternal plan sickness was meant to be a symbol of venial sin, just as death is a symbol of mortal sin. At any rate, the comparison has great merits and will be the theme of this chapter.

Death Worse than Sickness

No sickness or injury is pleasant or desirable; and the more serious the sickness or injury, the more unpleasant and dangerous it is. Yet, when compared to death, sickness is a small thing. For a person can be sick a thousand times and still live; but once he is dead, no earthly power can ever bring him back. Death is therefore a greater evil than a thousand injuries or sicknesses.

Mortal Sin Worse than Venial Sin

Similarly, a single mortal sin is a greater evil and does more harm to the soul than a thousand venial sins. For, whereas venial sin harms the soul, just as sickness harms the body, mortal sin snuffs out and completely destroys the spark of divine life in the soul, just as death snuffs out the life of the body. That is the reason why a serious or big sin is called *mortal,* a word taken from the Latin *mors,* meaning death. For mortal sin is the death of the soul.[1] Not that sin can destroy the natural life of the soul, which is immortal, but that it destroys its supernatural life: namely, its sharing, through grace, in the life and nature of God.

Sensible People Avoid Moral As Well As Physical Evil

No normal person is anxious to die or wants to be sick or injured, even if the sickness is just a toothache, or the injury just a sliver in one's finger. In the same way, no sensible person should want to commit spiritual suicide through mortal sin, or to inflict on his soul the spiritual injury of venial sin, even if the sin is but a vain thought or a little white lie.

---

1 "There is sin unto death" — 1 John 5, 16. See also James 1, 15, and Wisdom 1, 11.

Sin Is like Poison

Of the many causes of sickness and death, perhaps the one that serves the purpose of this chapter best is poison. For, whereas the natural causes of sickness and death are usually beyond our control, poison is something which a person can take into his body of his own free will, just as sin is something which a person admits freely and deliberately into his soul.

Three Classes of Poison[2]
Corresponding to the Three Classes of Sin

There are many different kinds of poison. Some poisons cause certain death, others merely make people sick, still others cause either sickness or death, depending on the amount taken. So it is with sin. Some sins cause spiritual death, others cause spiritual sickness, still others cause either spiritual sickness or death, depending on the seriousness of the evil admitted into the soul.

First Class of Poisons — The Most Deadly

Some poisons are so deadly that even a small amount will kill a person almost instantly. During World War II a poison so powerful was produced that a single ounce, it is said, could kill over 200,000,000 people. Needless to say, a person could not take a small dose of such a poison, for even the tiniest dose would kill him. Another example, not as striking as the above, but more familiar to everybody, is nicotine. In its pure, undiluted state, nicotine is so powerful that one-third of a grain,[3] much less than a single drop, can kill a man.

---

[2] This is not a scientific division. It is as valid as the division of things into strong, stronger and strongest; or into small, medium and large.

[3] There are 437.5 grains in an ounce avoirdupois. A grain is the average weight of a grain of wheat.

Spiritually speaking, some sins are just as deadly as the deadliest poisons. Examples of such sins are blasphemy, murder, and hatred of God.[4] Provided that a person has full knowledge and deliberation, such sins are always mortal. We know that a sin can be serious only when the matter involved is serious or is thought to be serious. In the case of these sins, the matter is always serious. A person cannot, for example, commit a small deliberate sin of murder; for every such sin is deadly, depriving the soul at once of its supernatural life.

Second Class of Poisons — Deadliness Depends on the Dose

Many poisons kill only when a larger dose it taken. A small dose merely makes a person sick, to a greater or lesser degree, depending on the strength of the person, the kind of poison taken, and the amount taken. Most poisons belong to this class. We take tiny amounts of various poisons into our bodies every day, but they do not harm us, at least noticeably, because the amounts are too small. However, if the amounts taken were to be gradually increased, we would begin to feel listless, then sick, and finally we would die.

Carbon Monoxide

A well-known example of such a poison is carbon monoxide, a very poisonous gas produced by the incomplete burning of fuel and sometimes present in tiny quantities in the air we breathe, especially where ventilation is poor. A small amount of the gas in the blood may make a person lazy and dull of mind. But as more of it is taken into the

---

[4] **Peccata ex toto genere gravia.** Other sins belonging to this class are: Despair, perjury (in the strict sense), breaking of the eucharistic fast, all forms of direct or deliberate impurity, etc.

body, the person begins to feel ill and finally becomes unconscious and dies.

Atomic Radiation

In our atomic age, we often hear of the ill effects of atomic radiation. We receive some of this radiation from various sources every day. Some of it comes from the earth, some from the air; and some, called cosmic rays, comes from outer space. In small quantities, the harm done by this radiation is negligible, but in larger quantities it is very harmful, even deadly.

Second Class of Sins — Mortal or Venial

Many sins are like the poisons we just mentioned. In larger doses, they are deadly spiritual poisons or mortal sins. In smaller doses, they are venial. In these small doses, they do the soul much harm by making it spiritually weak and sick so that it can more easily succumb to mortal sin, but of themselves they cannot deprive the soul of its supernatural life in God. The sin of theft belongs to this class of spiritual poisons.[5] Thus, to steal a dime would be matter for venial sin, but to steal many dimes would be matter for mortal sin.[6] It is the same poison in either case, but the dose received spells the difference between spiritual sickness and spiritual death.

Third Class of Poisons — The Least Deadly

The third class of poisons consists of those which harm the body in various ways, at least temporarily, but are not powerful enough to kill it outright. Perhaps the most familiar examples of such poisons are tobacco and alcoholic drinks.

---

[5] **Peccata ex genere suo gravia.** Other examples of this class of sins are: Intoxication, unnecessary servile work on Sunday, detraction, calumny, etc.

[6] No one can say with certainty just how many dimes constitute serious matter. Much depends on the circumstances. To steal the equivalent of a day's wages would seem to be serious matter.

[113]

Tobacco

The custom of using tobacco is so common that we scarcely pay any attention to it. We often hear of the many harmful effects of smoking, but we never hear of anyone dying just from smoking. We can say, therefore, that the tobacco habit is harmful but not in itself fatal. It is harmful because tobacco contains a deadly nerve poison, nicotine. It is not fatal, however, for two main reasons: First, the proportion of the poison in tobacco is small (2 to 8 per cent), and of this, only minute quantities actually get into the blood. And secondly, the body is able to destroy the poison and fortify itself with a certain immunity. Unfortunately, the body cannot destroy the poison fast enough or completely enough, especially if a person uses tobacco constantly and excessively. Moreover, the effort involved in getting rid of the poison is an added strain on the body, especially on the heart. As a result, the smoker is apt to suffer from indigestion, tobacco heart, nervousness, and other disorders. Some of these disorders may be only temporary, but others may be more permanent. The use of tobacco also disposes a person to more serious illnesses, such as heart trouble and cancer. Thus we have a fine example of a poison which we can consider as harmful but not deadly.

Alcohol

We know that alcohol can kill any living thing if enough of it is absorbed by the organism. We often hear of the harmful effects of using alcoholic drinks, especially if they contain much alcohol or if too much of them is used. Yet, we rarely hear of a person dying just from drinking wine, beer, or some similar alcoholic drink. Alcoholic drinks are not fatal of themselves because the human body is able to destroy or get rid of the alcohol quite rapidly. Even so, some alcohol remains in the blood for as much as thirty hours, doing at least some temporary harm to the body. Everyone knows of the many tragic effects of heavy drinking. But few people realize that alcohol temporarily paralyzes and even kills outright many of the white cells in the blood, making a person an easier victim of disease. From the records of Insurance Companies, we know that people who do not drink at all enjoy better health and live longer, on the average, than people who drink, even moderately. Thus we have another example of a poison which does not of itself kill, but which can weaken the body and prepare the way for more deadly enemies which can kill.[7]

(Before we pass on to the next part of our comparison, the reader will kindly note that we are not judging here the *morality* of smoking or drinking. Everyone knows that deliberate intoxication can be a serious sin. In this part of our discussion we are merely comparing the *physical* effects of tobacco and alcohol on the *body* with the *spiritual* effects of venial sin on the *soul*. In either case, some harm is done, but death does not follow, at least not as a direct consequence.)

Third Class of Sins — Always Venial

Spiritually speaking, some sins are like this third class of poisons. They harm the soul, but cannot of themselves destroy grace. Thus, they are always venial. White lies belong to this class.[8] As long as no harm is done and no

---

[7] We do not wish to imply that the moderate use of alcoholic beverages is never justified. On the contrary, a moderate use of alcohol may even be prescribed by a physician for certain ailments. In such a case, the good effects are calculated to outweigh the bad ones. From a social standpoint, truly temperate drinking can foster conviviality, which effect far outweighs the harmful physical effects. The Holy Scriptures condemn intemperance, but praise the moderate use of wine. Thus: **"Sober drinking is health to soul and body."**—Ecclesiasticus 31, 37.

[8] **Peccata ex toto genere levia.** Examples of other sins belonging to this class are: Intemperance in eating, impatience, vain thoughts, various excesses in things which are permitted, etc.

scandal given, a white lie is a venial sin, regardless of how big the lie may seem. Thus, a fisherman might modestly brag that the little minnow which got away was a full twelve inches long, or he might argue that it was a five-footer. The dimensions may vary considerably, but the sin is quite the same in either case.

The Skull and Crossbones

We often hear people say that looks are deceiving. This is especially true of some dangerous poisons. They look so nice. Some have a lovely pink color, others are bright green, still others, pure white, and so on. They could easily be mistaken for something good to eat or drink were it not for the skull and crossbones, the symbol of death, placed like a sentry over the poison, warning people to be careful, for danger of death is near.

The "Antidote"

Under this stern symbol of death, we find a short message of hope, entitled "Antidote." Usually the first words of this message are: Call a physician at once. The rest of the message states that the victim is to be given an emetic with lots of water to wash the poison out of the stomach by vomiting. Then something is to be given the victim to neutralize the poison taken, or to counteract its effects. If the poison was a strong acid, the victim is to be given an alkali, such as baking soda or chalk. If the poison was a strong alkali, the victim is to be given an acid, such as vinegar or lemon juice. Various other remedies may be prescribed and directions given to check the bad effects of the particular poison taken. The doctor, with his knowledge and experience, will know what else to do to best help the victim to recover.

Sin Is like a Treacherous Poison

So it is with the treacherous poison of sin. It often looks so nice to people. The world, the devil, and their own passions make it so. So they take it into their souls, thinking that it is a delicious treat which will make them happy. But once the poison is in their soul, they begin to feel pangs of remorse and to realize how bitter sin is and how harmful, even deadly, to their soul.

God's Laws Warn Us of Sin As the Skull and Crossbones
Warn Us of Poison

God does not want anyone to be poisoned with sin. If the devil sold sin in bottles, God would surely make him mark each bottle with a skull and crossbones to warn people that sin causes spiritual death. But since sin is an invisible thing, God must warn us against it in other ways. This He does through His Commandments and the laws of His Holy Church, which are like a spiritual skull and crossbones kept before our eyes by our own conscience whenever we are tempted to sin. We need, therefore, never be deceived, even though the poison of sin looks good to us, for our conscience always warns us in time, if we only try to obey it.

Antidote Against Sin

But if, in spite of the clear warning of conscience, a person does take the treacherous poison of sin into his soul, he should not delay or lose hope, but should consult at once the "antidote" against sin engraved in his own heart. First, he must beg Christ, the heavenly Physician, to come and heal him. Then he must avail himself of the spiritual emetic of Confession to wash the poison of sin from his soul. And finally, he must take the proper antidote to counteract the evil effects of sin in his soul. This antidote consists chiefly of prayer, sorrow, purpose of amendment, Holy Communion, and the practice of the virtues which are contrary to the sins committed. Thus, the sin of drunkenness should be overcome by abstinence; anger, by patience; theft, by giving alms, and so on.[9]

A Relapse To Be Avoided

After the sinner has recovered from the poison of sin, he should carefully avoid the occasions of sin, lest he be poisoned all over again. A relapse into a serious sickness is often very dangerous. So is a relapse into deliberate sin, especially mortal sin. For, the more a person sins, the weaker he becomes and the less conscientious, until it becomes very difficult for him to be spiritually well and strong again.

We Avoid Poisons of the Body But Not of the Soul

We shrink from the thought of deliberately taking poisons into our body, even in small quantities, because we are afraid of harming it. And what is our miserable earthly body when compared to our immortal soul? Yet we take the spiritual poison of sin into our souls every day, even deliberately, in countless small doses; sometimes perhaps even in fatal ones. And some people continue to live in the spiritual death of mortal sin, day after day, and even year after year, making little of it.

Flee from Poison

If deliberate venial sins are making you suffer from chronic spiritual poisoning, which makes you sluggish in loving God and weak in virtue, resolve at once to do some-

---

9 "Behold, Lord, I give one-half of my possessions to the poor, and if I have defrauded anyone of anything, I restore it fourfold." — Luke 19, 8.

thing about it. Flee from sin and its occasions as you would flee from poison ivy, from a nest of hornets, or from the fangs of a rattlesnake.

No Fun To Be Dead

But if, unfortunately, you should ever take the poison of mortal sin and die spiritually, do not stay dead. It's a tragic thing to be spiritually poisoned to death when one could so easily be enjoying the priceless gift of supernatural life in God. So, make an act of true and perfect contrition at once, and then go to Confession as soon as you can, so that Christ, the heavenly Physician, may cleanse the poison of sin from your soul, raise it up from the dead, and permit you once again to enjoy His presence within you, and to know the joy of living the life of a son of God!

"Moses accordingly made a bronze serpent and mounted it on a pole, and whenever anyone who had been bitten by a serpent looked at the bronze serpent, he recovered."

NUMBERS 21, 9

"And as Moses lifted up the serpent in the desert, even so must the Son of Man be lifted up, that those who believe in him may not perish, but may have life everlasting."

JOHN 3, 14-15

Chapter XII

"FROM DEATH TO LIFE"[1]

Natural Death

The difference between a living creature and a dead one is so great that the two can scarcely be compared. A dead tree can never bloom, or with its leaves shade us from the burning sun, or nourish and delight us with its fruit; it may not even be fit for lumber, but only for firewood. A dead dog is no longer a dog but only an empty shell of what was once a frolicking pet. A dead man, too, is no longer a man, but only a useless corpse. Death has erased every smile from his lips and snuffed out the light from his eyes; it has stilled his tongue to speech and stopped his ears to sound; it has even made his heart as cold and silent as a tomb, and has robbed his body of motion and his brain of the power of thought. Death is always a sad thing, even though it be the death of some small, seemingly useless creature. But the death of a human being is tragic, for it is the crumbling into dust of a dignity close to that of the angels.[2] For this reason, although through sin man deserved to die, God has resolved to "raise him up on the last day"[3] and make him live forever, for better or for worse, depending in the case of each man, on his merits.[4]

---

[1] "We know that we have passed from death to life." — 1 John 3, 14.

[2] "What is man, that Thou art mindful of him? Or the son of man, that Thou visitest him? Thou hast made him a little less than the angels; Thou hast crowned him with glory and honor; and hast set him over the works of Thy hands. Thou hast subjected all things under his feet."—Psalm 8, 5-7.

[3] John 6, 40.

[4] "And they who have done good shall come forth unto resurrection of life; but they who have done evil unto resurrection of judgment."—John 5, 29.

Unlike our mortal body, our soul can never die. Being spiritual, the human soul is of its very nature immortal, and no created power could ever destroy its natural life and existence. But, if we are in the state of sanctifying grace, our soul, besides its own natural life, is also endowed by God with a divine or supernatural life. And this supernatural life, unfortunately, we can lose through a single mortal sin. Mortal sin is, therefore, a form of death engendered in the soul, a bitter spiritual death which, though it cannot destroy the natural life of the soul, nevertheless leaves it shorn of the beauty and power of the life of God, just as physical death leaves the body shorn of the beauty and powers of earthly life.

If we could see and appreciate the unspeakable beauty, majesty, and glory of a soul graced with divine life, we could also understand the tragic state of the soul deprived of this life through mortal sin. But, as it is, only God can fully comprehend the pitiful state of such a soul. That is why He went to so much trouble to redeem us. We can at best only contemplate the tragedy of a human death and try to imagine a much worse tragedy occurring in a spiritual way in the soul.

Natural Death a Consequence of Spiritual Death

The death of the human body is not part of God's original plan for mankind.[5] It is rather a consequence of sin and a punishment for it. God would not have allowed the human body to die if man had not first chosen to die spiritually by depriving his soul of divine life. The decree

---

[5] "For God created man incorruptible, and to the image of His own likeness He made him. But by the envy of the devil, death came into the world." — Wisdom 2, 23-24.

of physical death in Eden came as a direct consequence of man's spiritual death through sin.[6] And the Son of God, who came to restore our supernatural life, also promised to restore our physical life through the resurrection of the body on the last day. In God's plan of redemption the two are inseparable. For as man lost these two lives through sin, the Redemption, to be complete, had to restore them both.[7]

"The Living God"

Only God can give the gift of life, and once it is lost, no power in heaven or on earth can bring it back, except the power of God. Living creatures can indeed *transmit* life according to God's laws, but they cannot create or produce it. Whether it be the highest angelic creature or the lowest microbe, the gift of life is exclusively God's gift. It is with good reason then that, in the Holy Bible, God so often calls Himself "the *living* God."[8]

Our Oneness with "The Living God"

Through the goodness and bounty of God, every living creature *has* life; but it would be incorrect to say that God has life—rather, He *is* Life. Every creature has the bit of created life which God has given it; but God is unlimited and eternal Life Itself. And it is in this that He makes us share when He gives us the supernatural life of sanctifying grace. Our created life of body and soul is something outside God, something which He has made. But the supernatural life which He gives us through grace is a share in

---

6 See Genesis 2, 16-17; 3, 17-19.

7 Though the damned will also be raised by Christ on the last day, their resurrection will not be a "resurrection of life" but rather a "resurrection of judgment," a state which St. John fittingly calls "the second death." We refer the reader to the last chapter of this book, where the resurrection of the just and of the wicked is treated at length.

8 The expression is used over thirty times in the Holy Bible; for example, "Thou art the Christ, the Son of the living God." — Matthew 16, 16.

[123]

His own intimate, uncreated life. Through it we are as it were incorporated into Him, becoming intimately *one* with Him, sharing, according to the limitations of our human nature, in the very life which entitles Him to be called "the *living* God."

No Two Alike

Sharing in God's divine life means sharing in His divine nature, perfections, and life-activity. It means sharing in His inner beauty, His goodness, love, happiness, wisdom, power and glory; though always according to the limitations of our nature and the measure of His giving. We notice this especially in the lives of His saints. Their wisdom, their power of miracles, their virtues — all proceed from their intimate union with God. Yet each one is different. The sun may shed its light equally on many objects in a given area, but not all receive or reflect the light equally. A mirror will reflect most of the light, so that it looks almost like the sun itself; but a piece of coal will remain black as night, even in the brightest sun. The same sunlight makes the sky blue, the leaves green, the snow white, depending on how each substance receives the light. So it is with human souls. Though many are God's adopted children, sharing in His intimate life and nature, no two are exactly alike and none can ever equal Him—nor can all of them put together. He is indeed "the living God."

1 CATERPILLAR TIME OF GROWTH  THE CATERPILLAR IS UGLY, SLOW AND CLUMSY. HIS EYES AND OTHER ORGANS OF SENSE ARE POORLY DEVELOPED. HE MUST EVER CRAWL ON HIS BELLY, LICKING THE DUST; EVER IN DANGER OF BEING CRUSHED OR ATTACKED BY HIS MANY ENEMIES. HIS HUGE APPETITE CAN SCARCELY EVER BE SATISFIED.	**1 OUR PRESENT LIFE** TIME OF MERIT | LABOR 	SICKNESS PLAGUES DISEASE	WARS 
ACCIDENTS 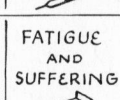	FATIGUE AND SUFFERING	CRIME AND SIN
SENSUALITY, INCLINATION TO SIN AND INORDINATE APPETITES ETC. 	HUNGER AND THIRST 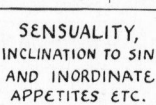		 
2 CHRYSALIS PERIOD OF QUIESCENCE 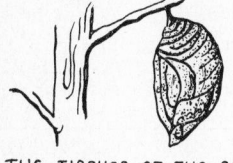 THE TISSUES OF THE CATERPILLAR DISSOLVE INTO A CREAMY SUBSTANCE FROM WHICH GOD FASHIONS A BUTTERFLY.	**2 AFTER DEATH** PERIOD OF REST  R.I.P. REST IN PEACE THE HUMAN BODY TURNS INTO DUST, WAITING FOR THE GREAT HOUR OF ITS GLORIOUS RESURRECTION.
3 BUTTERFLY FULLNESS OF LIFE  BEAUTY OF COLOR AND FORM. QUICKNESS OF FLIGHT. LIGHTNESS OF MOTION. NO GREED FOR FOOD. HIGHLY DEVELOPED SENSES OF SIGHT, SMELL AND FEELING. FEWER ENEMIES.	**3 AFTER THE RESURRECTION** FULLNESS OF ETERNAL LIFE  "AS ANGELS OF GOD IN HEAVEN." GLORY - HEAVENLY BEAUTY & SPLENDOR AGILITY - GREAT NIMBLENESS OF BODY SUBTILITY - A "SPIRITUAL BODY" FREEDOM FROM PAIN & DEATH EVERLASTING & UNCLOUDED HAPPINESS

Chapter XIII

THE RESURRECTION

Introduction

To speak of the remaking of the image of God in man's soul through sanctifying grace is to speak of only one part of man's eternal salvation. For man is also composed of a body which God originally intended to be immortal and incorruptible[1] and which He shall one day raise from the dead to live forever. A chapter on the resurrection is therefore a fitting conclusion to our little book on sanctifying grace. This becomes the more evident when we bear in mind that the condition of man's resurrection and immortality depends directly on whether he dies with or without God's precious gift of "life everlasting" which we call sanctifying grace.

Sin and Death Not a Part of God's Plan for Man

Sin and death came into the world through the fall of our first parents.[2] These two evils, which were brought into the world through the trickery of Satan, mean the total ruin of man; for sin ruins his soul by depriving it of the divine life of grace, while death ruins his body by robbing it of its natural life. Consequently, when Christ came into the world to save mankind, He had to undo these two chief effects of the Fall by destroying both sin and death completely and eternally.

---

1 "For God created man incorruptible, and to the image of His own likeness He made him. But by the envy of the devil, death came into the world." — Wisdom 2, 23-24.

2 See Genesis, chapter 3; Romans 5, 12.

[127]

Christ's triumph over sin and death, however, could not be the same in the just as in the wicked. In the just He destroys sin through sanctifying grace, and death through the glorious "resurrection of life." Grace and the resurrection thus mean the complete and perfect remaking or salvation of man, and the perfect triumph of Christ over sin and death. For grace remakes man's soul, despoiled by sin,[3] while the resurrection rebuilds his body, destroyed by death.[4] In the wicked, on the other hand, sin is destroyed by eternal damnation, while death is destroyed by the dishonorable "resurrection of judgment," so that, even in these unfortunates, Christ's triumph over sin and death is everlasting and complete.

Difference between the "Resurrection of Life" and

the "Resurrection of Judgment"

Jesus carefully distinguished between the "resurrection of life" of the just and the "resurrection of judgment" of the wicked.[5] For, although both the resurrection of "life" and of "judgment" mean a true return to life through the reunion of soul and body on the last day, there is an enormous difference between the kind of life the just shall enjoy and the wicked suffer after their resurrection—a difference as great indeed as between salvation and damnation.

---

[3] "But where the offense has abounded, grace has abounded yet more; so that as sin reigned unto death, so also grace may reign by justice unto life everlasting through Jesus Christ our Lord." — Romans 5, 20-21.

[4] "For since by a man came death, by a man also comes resurrection of the dead. For as in Adam all die, so in Christ all will be made to live."— 1 Corinthians 15, 21-22.

[5] "And they who have done good shall come forth unto resurrection of life; but they who have done evil unto resurrection of judgment."—John 5,29.

The glorious resurrection of the blessed, which St. Paul calls "the redemption of our body,"[6] will be a part of their eternal salvation just as surely as is the resurrection of their souls to divine life through grace and their ultimate glorification in heaven. And, on the other hand, though the wicked will also rise, the infamy of their resurrection will be a part of their damnation just as surely as the curse of God upon their wretched souls. For it is one thing to simply rise from the dead and quite another to rise unto the glory of the saints or the disgrace of the damned. Thus, when Christ raised Lazarus from the dead, He merely caused him to return to the natural earthly life which he possessed before he died. But when He raises the dead at the end of the world, they shall all be changed:[7] either endowed with the glory of the sons of God or covered with the shame of perdition, depending on whether they died with or without the grace and friendship of God.

Body and Soul Are One Complete Substance

To understand these things correctly, we must bear in mind that, in the living human being, soul and body form but one complete substance. In our everyday speech and writings, we often treat of soul and body as if they were two entirely independent things coexisting in the human being and even acting independently of each other. But this can be quite misleading. For the soul can do nothing without the body and the body can do nothing without the soul. The two are always interdependent and always responsible together for whatever the living human person may think, say, or do, whether it be good or evil. This condition will not be changed when body and soul are reunited at the end of the world. On the contrary, the union

---

6 Romans 8, 23.
7 1 Corinthians 15, 52-54.

between body and soul will be more perfect, and forever indissoluble. Body and soul will then share together, though each in its own way, in the reward or punishment which the human person merited while living on earth.

In This Chapter

In this chapter, we shall speak chiefly of the glorious resurrection of the just, merited for us by Christ and modeled after His own. But since, as we have already mentioned, the wicked shall also rise through the power of Christ, we shall devote a few paragraphs to that at the end of the chapter.

The Resurrection Is like a Beautiful Dream: Can it Be?

To every believing human heart, the thought of the resurrection is like a beautiful dream; a dream of the eternal youth of a body and a spirit which can never grow tired or old; a dream of unending happiness, serene, unclouded, and deep as a summer sky; a dream of walking with God down an endless pathway stretching through a paradise of gorgeous flowers which never wilt or fade or lose their fragrance; a dream of angelic song, of pure love, and bliss eternal. But, as is true of every beautiful dream, we may sometimes ask: Is it so? Can it really be? Not that we doubt Christ's word who has Himself put this dream into our hearts, but that it is too wonderful and too distant to seem real. In this regard we are like a person who, when suddenly overtaken by good fortune, pinches himself to make sure he is not dreaming.

A Dream of Spring in the Dead of Winter

How often, as a child, have I plodded over the cheerless, frozen acres of the countryside in the dead of winter—and dreamed of spring! All about me the dead earth, cold and

hard, seemed to ask: Will I ever live again? The deep stillness in the frosty air about me seemed to plead: Will the
birds and the bees ever come back to change my barren
stillness into music and song? But the only answer was the
low whisper of drifting snow or the rustle of a lonely
shriveled leaf, left unburied by wind and snow. How often,
when the biting wintry wind and stinging snow of the open
fields made youthful faces purple and numb, bringing tears
to the eyes, the young heart dreamed of gentle spring
breezes caressing the cheeks, and asked: Can it ever be?
Is spring real, or is it only a dream? How often young eyes
looked up at deserted, naked limbs of towering trees, dismal
and gray against the heavy sky, and asked: Where is your
color, your life? But the only answer was a faltering groan,
as a cold, stiff branch rubbed against another in the heartless wind which moaned through the forest. If one were
lucky, one might glimpse a lonely hare desperately fleeing
from the scene; or a scolding squirrel with chattering teeth;
or a snowy owl on silent wings searching for a shivering
mouse; or a downy woodpecker tapping on a tree and
getting only an echo in response. Everything else, as far as
the eye could see, seemed so hopelessly cold and dead. Even
the brooks were still beneath the ice. And the sun, if it
dared to shine at all, was so wan and pale, one could almost
look it in the face, and so weak that it might have been
framed in dainty crystals of snow.

A day seems so terribly long to a child. And the cold,
bleak winter, when the snow lay deep and the cold was
bitter, seemed almost endless. Little wonder that in the face
of such desolation, ruin, and death our impatient young
hearts asked: Will the earth ever come to life again? Not
that we doubted it, for we witnessed the wondrous marvel
of spring every year but that, in the cold stillness of winter,

spring seemed so unreal and so distant—like a lovely, impossible dream.

So, too, when we gaze upon the cold, still features of someone we have known and loved, we might ask: Will he (or she) ever live, walk, smile, and speak again? Not that we doubt it, but that it seems as unreal as a dream of lovely spring in the dead of winter.

Our Dreams of Spring Always Did Come True

Our childhood dreams always did come true—spring always did come. First, the sun grew stronger and climbed higher in the sky, while the shadows grew shorter and the wind lost its sting. Then the snowdrifts began to shrink, while the earth turned soft and brown, and the brooks began to gurgle again. Then the furry little catkins of the pussy willow began to glisten like silver in the sun, the braver birds announced their coming from the south, and the first uncertain notes of the peeper, a tiny frog, trilled from the swamp in the darkness of early evening. Slowly at first, then with ever-quickening pace, the dead earth was coming back to life again. The air gradually filled with sound and song, and the earth became ever warmer and greener. In the forest, the marshes turned a handsome deep green, crowned with the golden blooms of the cowslip,[8] while the higher ground was clothed with tiny pink Mayflowers,[9] hepaticas, and violets blooming in the thickening shade of the forest trees, now turning green with tender leaves. The fresh green meadows, too, began to fill with flowers of many kinds and colors and sizes, gorgeous in the sunshine, waving, swaying, and nodding gaily in the balmy breezes. Spring had come at last—the fullness of spring—where once the icy death of winter had reigned.

---

8 The marsh marigold.
9 The trailing arbutus.

So shall it be with you and me on the day of the great resurrection. Our dreams of eternal spring in paradise will at last come true, if only we are found worthy of it.[10] The icy grip of death will be gone forever, replaced by the glory of the resurrection and the everlasting life of the sons of God. Yes, it can be, for the Son of God proved it on the day of His own resurrection; and it shall be, for He has promised it.

How Shall It Be?

For ages past, whenever the hope of the resurrection has been mentioned or discussed, people have asked, to borrow the words of St. Paul, "How do the dead rise? Or with what kind of body do they come?"[11]

Mighty Oaks from Little Acorns

St. Paul answers this question by saying that when a seed is sown in the ground, it dies, but in its place there rises something new and different—a green, living plant. The same is true of the resurrection of the dead. The bodies we now have are, by comparison, like the common seeds we plant in the garden. But after they shall have risen from the dead, they shall be as completely changed as a seed that has become a living plant. Everybody knows the great difference between a seed and a plant. Let us consider, for example, a tiny carnation seed. It looks like a little, dark, shriveled flake of nothing useful. It is hard to imagine that such a seed could one day become a beautiful, fragrant carnation. Yet, as soon as we put it into the moist earth, this great marvel of nature begins to happen, slowly but

---

10 See Luke 20, 35.
11 1 Corinthians 15, 35.

surely. The same is true of every living thing which grows from seed, whether it be a new rosebush, or a sprig of grass, or a mighty oak growing from a tiny acorn: there simply isn't any likeness, and there is little proportion, between the seed and the living thing that grows from the seed.

"So also with the resurrection of the dead."[12]

So shall it be with us on the great day of our resurrection. Though our bodies will be the very same ones we have now, they will nevertheless be changed into spiritual bodies, so strong, so beautiful, so glorious, so excellent in every way that we shall always marvel that they are the same crude, clumsy, weak bodies we had while living in the world.

From Caterpillar to Butterfly:

Childhood Love of the Butterfly

One of the greatest enchantments in the life of a little child is the sight of a beautifully colored butterfly, flitting about in the summer sky, like a lovely runaway flower. With what glee we used to run after butterflies over the flowering meadows, when we were children. And when one finally alighted on a flower of its choice, we would quietly come up close to it, and, wide-eyed with wonder, we would watch it gracefully move its beautiful wings slowly up and down as it sipped the fragrant sweet nectar of the flower. With the simple faith of a child, we saw in it a masterpiece of color, grace, and beauty, fashioned by the delicate hand of God. To us a butterfly was a very special little creature, something midway between the lovely flowers upon which it rested, and the fairies which we thought hovered about in the air in which the butterflies lived.

---

12 1 Corinthians 15, 42.

Childhood Dislike of Caterpillars

Fond as we were of butterflies, we despised caterpillars. Little did we realize at the time that an ugly caterpillar was a beautiful butterfly in the making. As a butterfly, in our opinion, was something from fairyland, a caterpillar, on the contrary, was something from the lower regions. It was just an ugly "worm" whose only reason for existence was to devour good plants, to crawl into the wrong places and to make a general nuisance of itself. To our little minds, a caterpillar was a cousin of the snake, and a snake was a cousin of the serpent in Paradise—and the whole ugly lot of them was a part of man's punishment for sin. Consequently, we had almost as little sympathy for caterpillars as we had for sin itself. We especially disliked the tent caterpillars, which spun silken nests in the crotches of our favorite apple trees and devoured the leaves. Another type was the less common but more ugly tomato worm, a large green thing with a cruel-looking horn near the trailing end of the creature.

Childhood Discovery of the Chrysalis

I remember a cold October day in my childhood. It was just after the first killing frosts of autumn. The forests had already changed from the common green of summer to the rich medley of autumn reds and yellows, browns and purples. The open fields were brown and bare, except for the shocks of corn, the golden-yellow pumpkins still clinging to shriveled vines, the light green patches of cabbage, the dark green fields of winter wheat, and the dead and blackened potato vines at our feet. It was potato-digging time on the farm. The work was hard and the time was short; so everybody had to help. The long rows of potatoes were dug up with a special plow pulled by a team of horses.

[135]

The plow was rather inefficient, exposing only some of the potatoes to the chilly autumn wind. The rest had to be searched out with little hands, red with cold and dark with soil, groping and shoving through the soft mounds of cold, damp earth. But potatoes were not the only things our busy little fingers found in the dark earth. On this particular day someone found a very strange little object, about the size and shape of one of our little fingers. We had never seen anything like it before. Though the object was cold and still, we knew that it was alive, for it occasionally moved the tip of its abdomen slowly and stiffly. Its skin was tough and brown, divided into segments at the abdomen. It had no legs nor eyes nor mouth, but it did have what appeared to be the outline of small wings and something that looked like a long, thin, hard tusk along the underside. What the strange creature was, we could not guess. Soon all of the little workers were gathered around it for a conference, and one of the older ones recognized it as the pupa or chrysalis of a butterfly. We believed that all new life, whether it was a plant, a calf, or a kitten, came from the good earth. And here at last we had found a brand new butterfly, yet unborn, coming into the world. The dull little creature at once became the object of admiration and a kind of reverence. Little did we know that only a short time ago it had been an ugly caterpillar! Our only thought was a dream of a beautiful butterfly flitting about among the flowers some lovely day next summer.

Our Comparison

The wonderful way in which a caterpillar changes into a pupa and then into a moth or butterfly is a fine symbol of the earthly life, the death, and the final transformation of the human body at the resurrection. We can compare our present life to that of the lowly caterpillar; the period after our death to the state of the chrysalis; and our life after our glorious resurrection to that of the beautiful butterfly.

Every child who first learns that a caterpillar will some day become a butterfly is deeply impressed. An ugly caterpillar changing into a lovely butterfly! Why, it sounds like something from the story of Alice in Wonderland, or like something touched with the magic wand in the story of Cinderella or some other lovely fairy tale. If we did not see it happen, we could scarcely believe it. But because it is so common, we take it for granted, though it is a mystery worthy of eternal wonderment. The same can be said of the resurrection of the human body, dead perhaps for untold ages. That, too, seems so impossible, so unreal, so baffling to the mind and the imagination! Yet, we know that it will happen, because the same God who changes caterpillars into butterflies did transform and bring back to life His own dead body on Easter Sunday and has promised to do the same for us on the last day.

The Life History of the Butterfly:
The Caterpillar

There are many kinds of caterpillars in the world but none are pleasant to look it. Some are brightly colored but in a repugnant sort of way. Others are covered with short hairs which taste bad or may even be poisonous. Still others have a bad odor. A caterpillar is always a slow, clumsy creature, able to move about only by crawling on its belly, with its mouth ever close to the dusty ground. Its senses in general are poorly developed, though it does have great sensitivity to pain, and wriggles violently when attacked by a bird or by ants. Its eyes are not well developed and serve it poorly. It has two short feelers on its head, which help it to find its way around. Its only interest in the world is food and more food. Its greatest asset is its powerful mouth, with which it greedily devours large quantities of vegetation, often becoming a destructive pest in fields and gardens. Such an enormous appetite is bound to make the caterpillar grow big and fat. Soon it outgrows its own ugly skin, which bursts open at the seams; then out crawls the caterpillar dressed in a brand-new skin, more roomy than before, but just as ugly. The caterpillar then resumes its sole business of eating, until its skin is again too tight and has to be replaced. This happens several times until the caterpillar is fully grown.

The Chrysalis

When fully grown, the caterpillar suddenly loses its big appetite and finds a suitable place to change its skin for the last time. This time, however, its new skin is not the soft skin of a caterpillar, but the tough skin of a motionless, mummylike pupa, or chrysalis. It looks as if the caterpillar had died and had been sealed in a tight bronze casket. In fact, in the case of some butterflies and most moths, this mummylike creature is wrapped in a silken shroud which we call a cocoon. In the chrysalis, great changes begin to take place. All the tissues which the caterpillar had acquired through its industrious eating, now change into a soft, creamy substance. The caterpillar seems to have dissolved into a seemingly formless mass from which, as from a piece of soft clay, God now molds the marvel of a new creation. When the tough skin of the chrysalis at last bursts open, out climbs a butterfly: weak, unsteady, and damp, but complete and fully grown.

The Butterfly

Jesus once said that a grain of wheat dies in the ground in order to rise to a new and better life.[13] In the same way, we can say that the caterpillar perishes in the chrysalis in order to rise to the new and better life of the butterfly.[14] This, in fact, was the whole purpose of the caterpillar's existence. It ate so greedily only to acquire enough bodily tissue to be able to undergo this marvelous change. And its rapid growth was but a hastening to die to its lowly caterpillar life, to be buried in the deathlike stillness of the chrysalis, there to be completely transformed and to emerge at last as one of God's most lovely earthly creatures, with its jewel-like, velvet wings, its gracious form, and its quiet, enchanting ways.

If a Caterpillar Could Dream

If a caterpillar could think and be aware of its miserable condition and of the better life awaiting it as a butterfly, it would certainly long for the day of its transformation. Maybe it would climb to the uppermost leaf of a tree, shrub, or plant of its choice and begin to daydream of things to come. Perhaps it would strain its weak eyes and try to imagine how beautiful the world would look when viewed at last with two lovely compound eyes, each one containing thousands of simple eyes instead of the present six. Maybe it would wiggle its short, dull feelers, and try to imagine that they are the graceful antennæ of its future life, capable of delicate feeling, of fine hearing, and of keenly detecting the perfume of even distant flowers. Maybe it would sigh a great sigh as it thought of the day when all its ugliness would be changed into beauty, all its clumsiness into grace,

---

13 See John 12, 24-25.
14 Actually, neither the seed nor the caterpillar really dies. It is the same life appearing in a new form.

its slowness and weakness into swiftness and strength; when its short, creepy legs would be replaced with long, graceful ones; its heavy jaws and big mouth changed into a dainty sipping tube, coiled neatly under its chin; its greedy appetite for coarse, green leaves now satisfied with an occasional sip of nectar from a fragrant flower. How the day-dreaming caterpillar would yearn for the day when its fat, heavy body would be changed into a slender, dainty one; when it would at last be able to lift its face away from the dusty earth and soar into the pure, sunlit air, higher than the treetops, delighting in the colors and perfumes of a thousand different flowers! But since a caterpillar cannot know its lovely future, it never pauses to daydream about it, but spends all its days crawling about aimlessly and munching green leaves.

Man Can Dream of the Resurrection

Man, on the other hand, can and does know of his future transformation through the resurrection, for God Himself has revealed it to him. But, unfortunately, few people ever spend any time yearning for it, or dreaming about it, or even making themselves worthy of it. Most of them go about their daily lives like the lowly caterpillar, absorbed by the cares of the flesh and the passing pleasures of this world.

Qualities of Gloriously Resurrected Bodies

1. Subtility — "A Spiritual Body"

A flower can delight the eye with its form and color, or the nose with its fragrance. It can bring joy and inspiration to the heart, a smile to the lips, or perhaps a tear to the eye. Like a heavenly tonic, it can soothe the mind and ease the soul. A flower thus has certain marvelous powers for good which it did not have when but a tiny seed in the palm of one's hand. In a sense we can say that it is thus closer to the spiritual than when it was but a mere seed. The same is true of a butterfly. It has the power to delight and to inspire which it certainly did not have as a caterpillar. Its transformation in the chrysalis has given it a certain power over the mind and heart of man. Though it is still completely material, we can say that, in a sense, it too is closer to the spiritual than when it was a caterpillar.

The wonderful transformation which our bodies will undergo at the resurrection will be far more excellent than that of a seed changing into a flower or a caterpillar into a butterfly. St. Paul says that our gloriously resurrected bodies shall be "spiritual" bodies.[15] This means that, though still the same material bodies we now have, they shall nevertheless be so transformed by the power of God, and endowed with such marvelous gifts and powers, and be so completely subject to the soul, that, like our Lord's body after His resurrection, they shall be more like spirit than matter. Like Him, we shall be able to pass through closed doors and brick walls and any thickness of earth and stone as though they did not exist. No better words could be found to describe this wonderful transformation than the words of Jesus Himself when He said that those who shall be found worthy of the world to come "and of the resurrection from the dead," shall be "as angels of God in heaven."[16]

2. Glory

A person's face is like a little window through which we can see something of his soul. His face reflects whether he be good or evil, kind or cruel, happy or sad, calm or

---

[15] "What is sown a natural body rises a spiritual body." — 1 Corinthians 15, 44.

[16] Matthew 22, 30; see Luke 20: 35-36.

disturbed by passion.[17] This will be true in a much more excellent way in the resurrected bodies of the just. For, since their bodies will be more spiritual, the resplendent beauty of their souls as sons of God will shine through, glorifying them with its splendor. Our Lord tells us that "the just will shine forth like the sun in the kingdom of their Father."[18] No doubt, their bodies will be like that of our Lord when He was transfigured on the mountain in the presence of three of His Apostles, and "His face shone as the sun, and His garments became white as snow."[19]

The prophet Daniel says that the resurrected just "shall shine as the brightness of the firmament" and "as stars for all eternity."[20] All stars, however, do not shine with equal brilliance, "for star differs from star in glory."[21] So, too, not all the saints will be the same in glory and beauty, but each will have a glory of his own, depending on the merits of his earthly life.

3. Agility

A caterpillar is weak and heavy, clumsy and slow. It must ever stay close to the ground and can never crawl very far from the place of its birth. But a butterfly is swift and graceful, light and strong. It can soar high above the earth and fly perhaps for long distances.

In this world, our bodies, being subject to all the laws of matter, are also slow, clumsy, heavy, and weak. Our fastest airplanes must, to an ever greater extent, be controlled electronically, simply because our senses, our minds,

---

17 "A man is known by his look, and a wise man, when thou meetest him, is known by his countenance. The attire of the body, and the laughter of the teeth, and the gait of the man, show what he is."—Ecclesiasticus 19, 26-27.

18 Matthew 13, 43.
19 Matthew 17, 2.
20 Daniel 12, 2-3.
21 St. Paul, 1 Corinthians 15, 41.

and our muscles are too slow and too clumsy for the job. Compared even to the lowly ant, our bodies, in proportion to their weight, are very weak indeed. And like all material things, they are bound to the earth by the relentless force of gravity, as if by powerful elastic bands, so that the farther we get away from the earth, the faster and harder we must return, perhaps even at the cost of bruises and broken bones. This continuous pull of gravity, which we may call weight, makes it hard for us to work, to climb, or even to sit or lie for any length of time. And the effort to overcome gravity, friction and the inertia of matter, makes us tire very quickly.

Our glorified bodies, however, will be beyond the laws of material things. Like our Lord's body at His ascension, they will be free of the heavy bonds of gravity, and will thus be completely weightless. This, plus their superior strength, will enable them to move about and do things with great ease without ever getting tired. And being more spiritual, they will be gifted with a great agility, which will enable them to act with the swiftness and nimbleness of a spirit.

4. Freedom from Pain and Death

Caterpillars have many enemies. They live in constant danger of being poisoned, of being killed by birds, wasps, and certain insects, or of being stepped on and crushed to death as they crawl about helplessly on the ground. Little wonder that comparatively few caterpillars ever become butterflies. Once they do become butterflies, however, they are much safer, for they can avoid their enemies more easily. Thus the butterfly is in a sense further from pain and death than the caterpillar.

Our present life is very much like that of the poor caterpillar. We suffer from disease and accidents, from heat and cold, from hunger, thirst, and many kinds of pain, mental as well as physical; while the threat of death always hangs over us. But the gloriously resurrected bodies of the just shall "neither hunger nor thirst," nor suffer from heat or cold. "And death shall be no more; neither shall there be mourning, nor crying, nor pain any more," for "God will wipe away every tear from their eyes."[22] Our bodies, reunited perfectly and indissolubly with our immortal souls, will share in the incorruption and immortality of our souls.

The Resurrection of the Wicked

Not every seed dropped into the soil grows into a plant, for some seeds rot or are eaten by pests. Nor does every caterpillar change into a butterfly. Many, for example, are paralyzed by the poisonous sting of wasps, which then carry away their limp bodies to become the living food of future wasps. The ichneumon fly, in fact, pierces the body of the poor caterpillar and there lays its eggs. When the eggs hatch, the caterpillar becomes the host of tiny "worms" which devour its living flesh as they grow. Though the poor caterpillar remains alive during most of this time, it leads a wretched, sickly existence which should be called a living death rather than life.

So, too, though all men will rise from the dead, some will not rise unto everlasting life but unto everlasting death and destruction. These are the eternally damned in whom the beautiful dream of the resurrection never comes true as in the blessed, but changes into an everlasting nightmare of pain, remorse, and despair in hell.

The Glow of Hell-Fire Instead of Glory

Vice disfigures the face as well as the soul, even in this life. A thug is often known at a glance. Vice and corruption

---

[22] Apocalypse 7, 16; 21, 4.

will be even more evident in the resurrected bodies of the wicked. The ugliness of sin disfiguring their souls will show through their bodies in all its hideousness, while the eerie glow of hell-fire, permeating their bodies, will give them a frightful appearance. We do not know what effect the curse of an angry God and the disgrace of damnation will have upon them, but it will certainly be indelibly graven in their wretched souls and agonized faces.

The Immortality of the Damned

The wicked will indeed be incorruptible and immortal after the resurrection. But what a bitter and terrible immortality! To borrow a thought from the Bible, they "will seek death and will not find it; and they will long to die and death will flee from them."[23] Only one death will they be able to find—one which they shall never be able to escape—the eternal, living death of hell, "where their worm dies not, and the fire is not quenched,"[24] where "they will be tormented day and night forever and ever."[25] The immortality of the wicked, therefore, cannot be considered on a par with that of the just. It is rather a state of eternal dying and destruction which can never come to an end or be completed. St. John very appropriately calls it "the second death."[26] And Jesus says of it, "Be afraid of him [i.e. God] who is able to destroy both soul and body in hell."[27]

Other Qualities

Instead of the wondrous spiritual qualities of the bodies of the just, instead of their gracefulness, lightness, power, and exemption from the laws of matter, the bodies of the

---

23 Apocalypse 9, 6.
24 Mark 9, 43.
25 Apocalypse 20, 10.
26 Apocalypse 20, 6 and 14.
27 Matthew 10, 28.

wicked will be burdened with the opposite qualities. Their bodies will not only be a great burden to them, but the hopelessness of their state will make the burden greater. We know that even in this life when a person becomes mentally depressed, or loses hope or interest in life, he begins to suffer from emotional fatigue. He becomes listless and is always tired, while life itself becomes so great a burden that he may even entertain thoughts of self-destruction. How great, then, must this burden be in the utter hopelessness of hell, and how the bodies of the damned must weigh down their wretched spirits! Since such souls chose to be subject during their earthly life to the things of the flesh, their spirits must now be burdened and oppressed by the very flesh they sinfully loved and served.

Corn Smut—An Example

The mind and heart of a child, untouched by care and unsullied by sin and passion, can find many delights and bits of beauty in God's world which escape older people. Thus, a man considers his field of corn in terms of bushels and dollars. It means food for his stock and a livelihood for his family. But to a child, especially if the corn is dense and tall, it is a forest full of magic in which to hide and play. As children we found magic in the tall, green stalks; in the long, whispering leaves, whose feathery tips were seldom still; and in the lofty, flowering tassels. But most of all, we found magic in the tender young ears crowned with long, silken hair, sometimes greenish-white, sometimes red. As the ears swelled and grew, we would occasionally peel away some of their leafy covering to follow the progress of the glossy kernels, pale and milky, as they slowly hardened and turned into gold.

Not all ears, however, were graceful, firm, and sound. Some swelled unevenly, becoming almost as big as our heads, and broke through their coverings like ugly tumors. Older people called the growths smut, but to us they were ears that had gone bad. Instead of kernels of corn, a large, spongy, shapeless mass seemed to grow from the cob, slowly changing, as it ripened, from an ashen grayish-green to sooty black. At first we thought the ugly stuff was full of worms, devouring the ear; but not finding any worms in the growths, we began to use them as "hand grenades," heedless of the fact that Mother had to scrub our clothes by hand.

Our childhood ideas about smutty grain may not have been scientific, but, in a practical sense, we were quite right in judging a smutty ear as one which had failed; which instead of bearing grain, bore only an ugly mass of worthless matter, something to be despised and trampled under foot. Scientifically speaking, smut is a plant disease caused by a fungus which feeds on the plant as a parasite. The fungus not only robs the young kernels of their food, but actually replaces them with its lumps of sooty spores. It is thus a useless growth nourished by the plant itself in place of grain and bringing slow death to the kernels it infests. Smutty ears of grain are unfit for the use of man or beast, a total loss to the farmer.

Our Comparison

We can liken the risen bodies of the damned to smutty ears of corn. When a farmer sows grain in a field, he hopes to reap sound grain and not smut. If smut does develop, it is beyond his intentions or wishes. So, too, Christ wants us to be saved and to enjoy a glorious resurrection like His own. But if some people rise unto shame and punishment, it is only because of the smut of sin which corrupts and disfigures them in soul and body, making them spiritually dead and forever miserable, a total loss to God, to angels and men, and to themselves.

Conclusion

In a number of places in his writings, St. Paul expresses a deep yearning for the "glory of the sons of God,"[28] promised us by Christ. He says, "We ourselves groan within ourselves, waiting for the adoption of sons, the redemption of our body."[29] He knew that his soul would be glorified after death and would be perfectly happy with God. But he also realized that his salvation would not be complete until his body was also glorified. He wished that this could be done without the sad necessity of dying—that somehow he could be "clothed over" with immortality.[30] But since the glorification of his body seemed too distant and the only immediate door to glory was death, he preferred "to be exiled from the body and to be at home with the Lord."[31] But still, the final goal towards which he pressed and strained was the glorification of his whole person at the resurrection, which he called "the prize of God's heavenly call."[32]

Though St. Paul devotes many beautiful passages to the subject of the glorious resurrection of the dead, he barely mentions the resurrection of the damned. Why this silence?

---

28 Romans 5, 2.
29 Romans 8, 23.
30 "For we know that if the earthly house in which we dwell be destroyed, we have a building from God, a house not made by human hands, eternal in the heavens. And indeed, in this present state we groan, yearning to be clothed over with that dwelling of ours which is from heaven, if indeed we shall be found clothed, and not naked. For we who are in this tent sigh under our burden, because we do not wish to be unclothed, but rather clothed over, that what is mortal may be swallowed up by life."— 2 Corinthians 5, 1-4.
31 2 Corinthians 5, 8.
32 Philippians 3, 14. See also vv. 8-13.

Perhaps, if we were to ask him, he would say: Does a soldier in battle or an athlete in a race dream of the shame of defeat or of the glory of victory? So, too, the fervent Christian soul thinks less of the shame of damnation, and more of the glory of God's salvation of soul and of body. The true Christian denies himself and is willing to suffer the loss of all things, becoming like Christ in suffering, in order that he may attain to the glory of His resurrection. The good Christian puts to death the deeds of the flesh, and minds the things of the spirit,[33] ever striving to "live temperately and justly and piously in this world,"[34] in order to merit the "eternal weight of glory that is beyond all measure,"[35] the imperishable and everlasting "glory of the sons of God," bestowed upon those who finish this life in the blessed state of sanctifying grace.

[33] Romans 8, 12-13.
[34] Titus 2, 12.
[35] 2 Corinthians 4, 17.